Halloween Stories

A Halloween Adventure Story for Kids

(Adventure Halloween Story Picture Bedtime Book for Kids)

Bryan Stark

Published By **Darby Connor**

Bryan Stark

Halloween Stories: A Halloween Adventure Story for Kids (Adventure Halloween Story Picture Bedtime Book for Kids)

ISBN   978-1-7775276-3-1

Legal & Disclaimer

Table Of Contents

Table Of Contents

Chapter 1: Moment Of Silence

I'm not sure exactly what was more shocking to me, but the incident happened so abruptly that I was unable to figure it out. I'll try to clarify.

I've been struggling experiencing insomnia for several months. The doctor tried a variety of treatments but to no avail and I made the decision to keep going. However, the lack of sleep was draining me. I had become a depressing chaos during the day, and at about 6 pm getting ready for sleep.

I'd fall into bed around 8 p.m. and hoped in vain that this was the time I would sleep but then my mind would tell me "nope, not yet." My eyes would flutter wide and I'd be to think. There was nothing special to think about, no worries and no worries. Nothing significant--just thought about things. For example, I had plans for the upcoming day, which probably wouldn't be happening since I lay asleep. That's it was a long time of sleeplessness.

The initial surprise was when I was awake, which meant I was indeed to sleep. Wow! The second part shocked me. I was able to see myself rolling into the skies.

What is the view from the sky?

In my attempt to understand the situation, I was able to take a look around and noticed fiery pieces of debris and something that looked like people falling down to the ground with me. I turned my head down, which was where I was heading--and saw rock and water.

In putting together the little bits of my mind that I could gather, I came to the conclusion that I must have been suffering from a terrible nightmare or, that somehow, I'd landed on a plane that been destroyed, and was headed towards the brink of end. Naturally, the initial thought was the most appealing which is why I shut my eyes hoping to awoke.

The breeze whipped my clothes and hair all around my body. The feeling was real- but aren't dreams real even when you're experiencing these kinds of dreams? My eyes were opened again. The water and the rocks began to move closer in the second. Then I noticed individuals hitting them and then dying on the rocks, or at the very least, it appeared like the case.

I felt the warmth of fiery parts of the plane whizzing past me as they sped towards the ocean. It was hot when they struck the ocean. My ears were able to hear the same sounds, and then I could hear screaming, but not mine. I was strangely quiet. It was because it was a nightmarish dream. Surely.

I went in and was swept down. It was a long, slow descent. This is the perfect mess that I've pictured myself getting into. I wanted to kick myself but my skirt got caught within my legs. I pulled it apart in order to free it. I reached for my hands and arms in order to get myself back up, but was that sufficient?

I was almost out of breath. I started swallowing some water. I was pushing against something, a rock I had guessed. I pushed harder. I was pulling and pulling my hands and arms. I ran out of air. I wasn't going to be able to make it. But it was fine, since it was just a dream and I'd be awake anytime soon, and probably prior to drowning. Right?

I could make out the lights above me. The sun, I'm thinking. Because I don't recall traveling on a plane I definitely wasn't able to remember the exact moment of the day. Then I saw the sun, and I swam and pushed toward the light. until I ran out of air.

It was then that I just floated. It was so relaxing. So peaceful I was happy that the nightmare of the plane's explosion been over, and that I didn't have to get out of that sea. What was the ocean, anyway? But, that's not a problem at the moment. I was able to go back to the bed. It was back into another night.

After five days the funeral took place five days later. The sermonist spoke over me and the rest of the passengers who took off on the plane that was headed toward Spain at that moment. Every single passenger as well as every crew member died. My family was not there and no one was around to grieve my loss. I didn't reveal to anyone that it was simply a fantasy.

The NTSB, the Coast Guard and even the Navy were enlisted to find all components of the plane that was destroyed in the blast. A few were located so deep under the ocean that divers had been sent to descend using rigs and pulleys to drag them back closer to the surface to find out what went wrong.

The TSA scoured the videos from the check-in points by the TSA in search of any indications of terror, or any indications of any missing information. The theories were circulated by various media outlets over the course of days and weeks. It was likely that someone put things in their luggage that was checked into the cargo compartment underneath the aircraft, according to reports.

Everyone shared their prayers and thoughts to God as they lit candles for the time in silence. While the news cycle began to move on to other intriguing news and the news cycle moved on. There were always new and important stories to read.

It didn't matter at the in the end. There were a hundred and thirty-two lives destroyed, which included mine, even though I had no idea about the fact that I had thought it was an illusion. I'm still unable to recall why I had been in the plane heading to Spain. Yet, I recall seeing the lighting. I do remember running towards the lighting.

I lay on the earth, not able to see a light and then finally, I was able to rest in peace. I believed that those who died that day would have the same luck. the light and swim toward it. I could sleep more tranquil knowing that at the end.

A Moonlit Rose

By Rachel Ann Michael Harris

AIDEN SPOKE, DUPLING OVER. The bouquet fell out of his hands when he fell on the table in the hall scattered the flowers and scattering picture frames onto the floor. He threw his hands out in the air, fingers stretched wide when he tried to squeeze his hands.

No. No,

not right now.

The light of the full moon came in through the window creating an inscrutable glowing shadow over him. Every muscle tightened, and stiffened, Aiden fought the change that was sweeping over him.

Hair grew on his arms and hands. The legs bent and curled into the form of an animal's hindquarters. The length of his nose increased to an snout and his teeth slammed into fangs as the dog growled.

The ears moved between his ears. Through a loud bark, and growl Aiden fell to his front feet.

He hung his head low and exhaled. The low growl grew deep into the lining of his throat. The glass that shattered under his feet shuddered while he walked and the sharp edges cut the paws of his. Eyes watering, Aiden howled. He snatched at the roses. Aiden ran across the hallway towards the front door. He left blood smears across the photographs of him as well as Tara as well as his "Happy Birthday" card he'd held with his roses.

TARA got a ride outside of her Apartment building. Aiden told her he'd come and come and pick her up, however the time was over an hour. He sounded so happy when he spoke to him. Perhaps more than she was on her birthday. It was a bit odd for him to arrive tardy. After pulling out her phone she thought about making a call to him.

The leaves rustled, and the branches broke. Tara spun around. Two eyes shined through the trees. The dog, which looked like a wolf, slowly entered the glow of the streetlamp. The dog was gray with matted fur, and had the long white fangs that were stained by red. Three roses were locked inside his jaws.

Tara was hesitant to move away, and then he paused. The the blood on his teeth looked similar to . . . the one he had. The rose thorns caused pain to his gums and lips, making them bleeding. The man seemed sad; his face hanging open, his eyes numb, and tail dropping. He threw a slight whine.

A portion of her would like to go running. Half of her thought that she was supposed to stay. What did this thing mean and why did it appear here? The phone was on her desk. Do she need to call anyone? Under the light of the moon's fullness, Tara and the beast was at a dead end and the autumn breeze blew through the trees, as they were contemplating the same issue.

"What's wrong with you," the neighbor blurred. "You never say hello to me. Do you feel stuck or some other reason? Would you consider yourself too nice to greet you?" Her voice was increasing as she spoke. Stephanie was scared she'd cause trouble for the other tenants. she could not afford to let anybody question why she was leaving during the night.

"Sorry, Ethel, I have to run to the store and get some milk," she said as she tried to hide from the curious woman.

"Well, why didn't you say so?" Ethel shouted. "I've discovered a bottle inside my fridge. If you'd like to say hello, I'll hand you a drink!" She belched, and left the smell of old booze as well as old broad throughout the corridor.

Stephanie placed her hand towards her nose. The scent was horrible. She really needs to cut down on her drinking. "That's okay," she declared, turning her back to the elevator. "I don't want to bother you."

However, Ethel wasn't being a good sport about the same experience. "What do you mean, my milk just isn't enough for her high status? Could that be the reason?" Her voice was higher than ever before, and Stephanie was aware that she had to respond immediately.

"You know what Ethel, I would love to borrow some milk from you, can I come in and get some?"

Astonished by the change in attitude, Ethel wasn't sure what she should say. Stephanie was able to take advantage of her disorientation and grabbed the woman's arm and steered her to the back of the room. She shut the door behind them before letting loose her arms.

She smiled softly at Ethel and asked "About that milk?"

"Of course," Ethel declared. "Let me get that for you."

"Why Thank you! I'm grateful that you saved me the expense of a night out. I don't like going out in the evening, and I'm not required to!" She grinned at the woman extremely confused and drunk.

Ethel was trying to pour milk out of the carton into a glass. Her mind was so preoccupied with not spilling any of the milk, she didn't hear Stephanie follow her behind. Stephanie struck Ethel across the face by kicking her with the family Bible which landed her on the floor. She lay down on the ground to feel her pulse. She was relieved to see she was living. The syringe was removed from her purse and then injected Ethel. "That should keep you quiet for a minute."

Stephanie was looking through the room. There were alcohol bottles throughout the room. There were bottles of alcohol, but little other. In a brief moment she was sad for Ethel however, she was thinking of her daughter and how happy she would be to receive an exciting sweet treat. She'd do whatever it took to ensure that her daughter was happy. That's her kind of mother she was.

As she flung the woman unconscious beneath her armspits and dragging her to her knees before she carried her on her powerful shoulders. The woman was stunned by how strong she had become since looking for the food of Eve. Her athletic background was never her kind, and had always been an avid reader who preferred being in the house. However, she was a woman to behold! She was tough, she was intelligent, and was unstoppable.

The girl looked through the window that was in front of the door to Ethel's. There was nothing moving within the hall. The door was opened a gap and began to listen. The only sound was Ethel's breath. Perfect. She reached inside her bra and took out the key to her apartment. The key fell in between her hands.

She left her apartment and slammed the door to her. Her eyes wandered around the hall in search of any movements, or any issue. Nothing. She swiftly walked along the hallway to get to the apartment's door. The key was inserted into the lock but it wasn't able to go completely in. When she moved Ethel in order to provide herself with an extra leverage in her hand, she could hear the elevator's motor begin to rev up.

"Shit, shit, shit, shit, shit," she said with a sigh. She turned the key with dismay, and nearly screamed when it suddenly came back to the floor and turned the knob. The woman entered her home and closed the doors behind her before the elevator landed on the floor. She stood and stared through the window while the doors opened.

An individual stepped out from the elevator. He went straight to the front door and approached. He sat, his with his hands in pockets looking for her answer. The woman was weighted down on her back and straining her muscles and Stephanie felt nervous sweat run down her back however she remained in her position.

The man knocked on the door. He then shouted, "Hey you drunk old broad, answer the door!"

The door was open and it was far enough into the hall that Stephanie could not discern. One man was shouting "Hey Jackass! People sleeping! Stay awake!"

The person at the door of Ethel turned the other person into like a bird before banging on the door once more. At this point, the person from the house walked up to him, and Stephanie saw young, with muscular arms, sporting a military cut. "Are you deaf? People try to fall asleep."

As he walked away from the door of Ethel the man who was first in line was able to take a look at the boy and took a deep breath. The man realized that this wasn't a person who he would want to play with.

"Fine," he said with a smile of defeat. "I'm leaving. However, I'll be back." the man screamed at Ethel's front door.

When the guys left, one taking the elevator and one returning to his home-- Stephanie took a step out of the way exuberantly. This could have been better had I made it up! She thought. Then there'd be a reason to suspect Ethel's disappearance is discovered.

Then she turned around and threw Ethel on the floor. It was a shame, as her back and arm were hurting after having to hold Ethel and sitting for such a long time; however, the work wasn't over until. It was impossible to rest until Eve was fed.

She walked into the small box at the heart area. She pulled the pull cord of the only lightbulb that was hanging over the top. The light reflected onto a tiny space covered with Tarps. In the shadows of the tarps, there were soundproofing panels that she'd constructed by herself.

As Eve consumed food, she produced noisy slurping sounds. They were at first not so bad. However, now at 6 months old, her noises became a source of concern. Stephanie designed the room to ensure that Eve could eat her meals in peace and no one would be hearing anything. She was unsure of how this would be able to work in conjunction with Ethel. A majority people who ate "food" had been newly dead, so brimming with chemicals that they were unable to be heard, or in recent times, taken out of the freezer.

Stephanie dragged Ethel into the container she then shackled her in a way that resembled hogs, and tied her up with her feet and hands on her behind. Ethel began to wake up and agitate, so Stephanie realized she must get her to the door as quickly as she could. The enclosure was not noiseproof until the lid was shut.

The woman tied the knot, and then quickly pulled the scarf and put it around her neck. It was an attractive scarf with a gorgeous blue silk with a floral design. It was a great gag, she thought. She put the edges of the scarf inside Ethel's mouth, and tied the two ends to her head.

While Stephanie got up and wiped her fingers on her jeans, Ethel turned her head toward her. The eyes of Ethel were frenzied when she tugged on her shackles, trying to comprehend her circumstances.

Stephanie was seated and turned to look Ethel into the eyes of Ethel. "Next time, if someone doesn't feel like saying hello to you, let it go," she suggested. And then she laughed. There was never going to be a second moment for Ethel.

When she heard a tinny sound in the background, Stephanie turned and looked at her daughter's gorgeous golden eyes that were adorned with swirling blood red sparkles. "Mommy loves you little girl," she reached down to touch her little girl's forehead. "I gave you a sweet snack, sweetheart. You can find it right there." she pointed out the feeding area of her daughter.

Eve turned her attention to her mother and smiled the biggest smile. A row upon a row of small tooth-like, clean white teeth sparkled in the sunlight. After that, she stepped in the tin box.

Ethel was in a panic and was running around trying to be loose. As she was able to see the little girl and sat down for a few seconds. Stephanie was able to watch her face swell with horror as the eyes of Eve and mouth echoed within the woman's brain soaked in gin.

Stephanie shut the door to the side of Eve and hoped that the woman's screaming would not get past the noiseproofing. Feeling tired but content by herself, she lay on her bed to relax as Eve was eating dinner.

Chapter 2: A Spiritual Feast

The tiny HOUSE was beginning to sleep into the darkness for the night.

The warm sun was about to fade behind the mountains that bordered the valley of trees. In the past, she'd stuffed the fire with cut wood in order to keep away the chill that was set to creep on the evening that was coming towards. The loaves that were rounded from baking bread that were rising beneath the white cotton sheet could be seen on the table waiting to bake.

The woman walked out of from the front door and on the porch and went into the backyard and walked around the yard to look over the chicks. The snow hadn't yet got too thick, however she sat down within the coop in order to ensure that everything was in order and found it to be. They were in a huddle and seemed to be asleep. The woman stood up and grabbed her lantern that she carried along, in order to help her get light.

She called her dog and she walked them back to the house The smell of stew cooking away in the wood fire pit heating her while she went into. Making bread for her oven made her dog's meal bowl. After he had eaten the food, she relaxed on her chair in a rocking position and started knitting with the help of a lantern for her source of light.

The pace of time was slow in this tiny farm which was great. She was grateful for the dog, and for everything she's ever dreamed of. There was a constant rhythm in the valley and she was a piece of it. She rocked as she knitted, and her dog finished his meal and wandered to the braided rug in front of the rocker, careful now about his tail, having had it rocked on, once-- unintentionally of course.

The bread was almost finished, so she cleared her table. A spoon, a crockery bowl as well as a dish to serve the bread and a butter stick and an ice-cream knife. The candle was lit out of beeswax, which she had collected from her beehives, and then found a jar of honey from the same hives. She set it out on a table. She filled her glass, put it on the table and slid it over the bench and laid the cotton on top of the bowl.

The woman was getting ready to get the bread from her mouth as her dog started to sniff the front door, and his tail began to move. It was clear that boots were on the floor. Then she went to the door. It was not frequently that people find them here. she wasn't expecting any. The door was opened, being aware that her dog would notify her if they sensed danger. she was not concerned.

A teen, dressed with a down parka, topped with a cap sporting snow boots with a huge backpack was sat on the patio.

"Ma'am? I've wandered off path and got in a haze. Would you mind if I asked for drinking water? I've ran out of water and I'm getting so thirsty that I do not think I'm able to go further. This would be extremely nice of you," he said, in a shiver.

"Goodness!" she said. "Please bring yourself into. You're freezing. Let me assist you." She opened her backpack to check and found he was carrying a walking stick. They were both placed on a bench near the entrance to the house. He took off his hat and placed it on his chest, like he pledged some kind of sacred thing to her. The truth is, it appeared that way. The man was simply touched to be treated as an invited guest rather than as an criminal. "You seem like you could need some food in addition to this water. We're getting ready to cook freshly baked bread and stew and bread. Can I make the bowls for you as well?"

"Gosh this sounds fantastic. Is it sure that you're not in problem? Have you got enough? Don't take this if it's all that you've got," He stated.

"I don't think I would give it away if I didn't have it available to offer. Let me set down a bench in your place."

He threw off his jacket and gloves, then took a long look at the food while she placed a bowl in front of her at the table. She laid out a dish with a delicately wrapped cotton cloth next to the spoon. He watched her pour the rich stew that was bursting with beans, tomatoes and other herbs, into bowls. She also watched while she cut the bread that was warm and fresh freshly baked. Two slices were placed on his table and another slice over hers. She served him butter as well as the honey and he ate both. She put water in an ice-filled pitcher before placing the bowl on the table. She then began serving him a glass, as well as her own. He ate the dinner and his appetite was evident.

It was a slow and respectful meal taking note of all the effort she'd put in preparing the veggies and herbs that were in the stew. She felt thankful for the sun and rain, which had provided food to them. While she spread honey over her toast, she was thinking of her honeybees, and how much they enjoyed the trees of sourwood. They added a flavor for the bees to make the most delicious honey.

He had finished his meal and was ready for a second serving after he realized that she had not finished those first bites. She noticed that he was thirsty to have more and which is why she stood up, and replenished her bowl, plate, and glasses.

He continued eating because it was time to eat.

"Aren't you hungry?" He said.

"Oh yes, I am," she replied.

"Is this you? Since it's delicious to me,"" he added.

"Yes, I think it's very good," she stated.

"But you are eating it so slow - like you really don't want it."

"I take my food slowly as I like to enjoy every bite and remember my efforts into it, the bees did, and that the sun, rain and earth created - all to bring me this tiny dinner. In order for me to take the enough time to recall all of the things I have eaten, I need to consume food slowly," she said, her voice quiet.

He was sitting there. He was young taking a stroll through the forest. The idea was one he believed was a cool and trendy idea to take part in. He'd purchased the down parka, the designer shoes, the most expensive walking stick, and the huge backpack. But he had not bought anything or worked on all of it. His parents purchased it for him, just similar to how they'd covered every other thing throughout his lifetime.

In that instant the man realized that he'd not ever thought about what the origins of everything. He'd not even considered the fact that the meals his parents purchased in the grocery store had to originate somewhere. He'd never considered being thankful for the effort that was required to bring food items to this point. He had not thought about the sun, the rain, nor the watering required. He'd never even seen homemade bread before, let alone eaten it.

The strange, mysterious woman, whose identity was not even known--and who did not even ask to know his name had invited to her home and provided him with food through the work by her own hands, as well as the hives and gardens.

He looked around at the empty bowl, and at the crumpled crumbs on the plate. He was full of food, however, he was feeling oddly empty. He realized he'd left something out there, somewhere.

He looked at her. "You seem like you're in need of some time off. If you lay on the ground next to the wood fire I've got an extra cushion and quilt and it should be warm enough to enjoy a nice rest. It's possible to benefit from it." she told me.

"Yes it sounds good. I'm grateful," he said. It was awe-inspiring that the woman was willing to let him rest there and yet simultaneously it was not all that awe-inspiring. He sat and watched her walk across the stairs made of wood to an unspecified loft. Her descent was accompanied by pillows covered with white fabric and an enthralling quilt that was adorned with intricate embroidery stitching.

"It was made by my grandmother," she told me. While he lay down on top of the fireplace her quilt was laid on top of him. What he last saw when his eyes were shut was her in her chair, rocking with her knitting. Her dog snuggled up beside her, with its tail snuggled underneath his body. When he sank to sleep and fell asleep, he heard her gentle singing. He couldn't identify the song but the tune sounded familiar.

After waking up a few hours after, she was not there. The wood stove was restored to its original state. His backpack was placed next to the rocking chair with a walking stick, hat and gloves. glove and hat. A lump was found in the backpack and the man took it out. There was a bag of paper filled with sandwiches that were made of homemade bread with honey, peanut butter and honey. Also, there was an inscription.

"Savor the moment."

The dog's name was not known however, he was determined to leave a message for her and so called her name however there was no response or even a bark. The dog was gone as well. With a shrug, he left the front door.

The sun was shining brightly in the dark house It was able to blind him for a short time. Then he returned to the house, and was shocked to find it was old and broken down, and appeared abandoned. The door to the screen was hung by a hinge that was on the bottom, and it moved slightly in the cold air. The wooden steps had been damaged and he'd need to be cautious when stepping down.

He thought about if it could have just been an illusion. He pulled out his bag. The sack of paper was in there. It contained a note. He was confused, and went to his room. The bizarre quilt was still in the spot it was when he left, however it was damaged as well as awashed in mouse droppings. He went up the steps with care to stay clear of the steps that were broken However, there was nothing up the stairs. He went back to his feet in shock. He went back outside. There was nothing to garden about and no chimney to wood stove or the smell of smoke. There were just some broken bricks that were crumbling down to the floor.

The sun was shining brightly and shining on the man. While he surveyed the surroundings at the sun, he realized that the sun wasn't shining on the snow that had fallen the previous night. There were also some trees that were green, which he had not had before. Then he walked toward them, and the lights appeared to follow his footsteps. They were huge, reddish-orange berries at the base of the tree - he'd not seen anything similar before.

He retrieved one and chose the fruit up. Then, with a smile, he put the piece on his tongue. It was delicious! He continued to pick, which filled the pockets of his pants. He began to think about whether the bush would fill with berries during the winter months, but then the thought stopped him. Is it a good idea to question the situation and then stop for at a point and be thankful to have it? He sat in the light of day and placed a couple of fruit in his mouth. His with his head bowing. He walked back towards the crumbling cottage that was sagging into the earth directly in front of him He sighed and then shook his head. He was now ready to leave.

He went on to begin the walk in a renewed state of thanksgiving. It could have been an accident, but maybe not. Whatever the case, it was a valuable lesson that he will never ever forget. It was no longer a matter of measuring the distance he walked in. He would focus upon the tree and its barks as well as the clouds, snowflakes; the bushes, and fruit; the sounds of creatures scurrying around; the concealed creatures; birds calling over the horizon and trying to build nests. It was a way to be grateful for the things he usually didn't think about - the carefully folded cloth, the earthenware dish, home-cooked food, all of which were overlooked by him in his attempt to be a better person.

Chapter 3: The Witch's Halloween Surprise

The fairy lights swayed overhead in a pulsing rhythm of the beat. The electronic dance track did not coincide with the ballroom's formal decor But wasn't Halloween a time for giggling?

I shook Kai's hands as I walked across the flooring. All thoughts went out of my head, except following his direction and feeling his hand. He whipped me away from him and then whipped my back with such force that I crashed on his torso. His hands swung around my waist and kept me against his.

His eyes were only two inches from mine. Did he intend to make me kiss him before everyone at school, as well as the whole Faerie Court? The white fur grew from his cheeks. The lips parted in the form of a smile and revealed the sharp edges of his teeth. Fox ears of red and white appeared through his hair, ruining the hairstyle that went with the James Bond tux.

I turned away from him with dismay. Stupid kitsune. He knew I'd just touch his face. I didn't want to stand acquaintance with someone that was akin to the animal.

Kai smiled and tipped my legs by his tail. "You don't like my costume, witchling?"

My hands were placed over my skirt to secure the dress, making sure the pirate did not try to pull the dress up. "It's not a Halloween costume when you look like that every day."

He looked at his watch. "C'mon, don't they say Agent 007 is a fox?"

"That's not what they mean!"

The music ended the two couples we were dancing with stopped and began to come into the room to dance with us. Glen and Ashleigh two of the Faeriekin, were clad in formal attire and adorned with masks. Ashleigh wore a blue and pink butterfly ballgown, and a mask that had the look of autumn leaves on her head. He was wearing a pumpkin-orange doublet, a pair of trousers that had gold trim, and the green leaf hat. He held her hand as is the appropriate manner for a couple who is engaged.

Heather and Anil were dressed in modern attire. Heather and Anil, both just like me, wore the white dress and angel wings to match her pale skin color and dark hair. She was scheduled to go on an evening date with Anil who was a snake. From waist-to-tail, the snake was green however, he was wearing the red color of his jacket, and the yellow scarf which might look like the clothes of a character from a video game. The two stood in awkward silence like they didn't understand how to behave.

"Let's take a break," Ashleigh stated. She threw Glen's arms down and grabbed the two girls. "You boys go get us some apple cider."

Glen bowed. "Of of course, it's my girl. I'll be back." The man left the scene, and Kai and Anil were forced to follow his footsteps.

Ashleigh led us to the space in which we could gather with each other in privacy. I was leaning forward in a smug smile. "So Heather, tell us all you know about. What's going on for Anil?"

Heather smiled. "Um, I don't know."

Ashleigh turned to me. "Gee, Rosa, why don't you tell us how things are going with Kai?"

My turn was to blush. "Well do you know ..."

I was unsure of why the I didn't know why things were difficult. Once I was no longer free from the constant surveillance of my mother I was able to date anyone I liked. Because we've kissed before, Kai should know that I was attracted to the guy. Although we had been dancing in the evening there was nothing mentioned to establish our relationship.

My companions were looking at me. I said, "I think that we're two of us unsure which one should be the first to move. ..."

Ashleigh looked at her partner with a smile. "I'll see if I can get you two some alone time."

The boys returned carrying small glasses of apple cider in each of their hands. I could smell the warming spice when Kai handed me a cup.

Ashleigh grasped Glen's arms. "Thanks. Hey guys, did you notice the jack-o lanterns in the contest to carve pumpkins?" She winked at me. In a flash, she swiftly moved the group off, leaving Kai and I gazing at each other.

Kai got close. "Hey, Rosa, would you like to go for a walk in the garden?"

I smirked at him with happiness. "Yeah, sure."

Our cups were quickly drained and put them on the table. Kai was kind enough to offer me his arm and I cuddled with Kai. Do I have a big opportunity?

The garden was gorgeous The garden was stunning, with twinkling lights draping over the gazebo, and the full moon glistening overhead. My costume for the pirate was slim, but Kai's warmth helped me stay cozy. Kai stood in a gloomy corner before turning to look at me before reverting back to his human body.

"Rosa I have something I've wanted to convey to you. ..."

My heart pounded. The man was much more attractive than an actual human. "Yes?" I breathed.

There was a rustle in the bushes in the bushes behind us. Kai took my arm and pulled me away. "Look out!"

I attempted to turn around to look at what was going on and I managed to fall through my pirate boot and land on my back. I looked up and saw an enormous golden dragon's head hanging over me. The protector! What was I doing to make her angry this time?

There was a problem, but there was something wrong. The head was way too small and the remainder of the guardian dragon's body could not fit into the space. My eyes widened, trying to catch a clearer view into the darkness. The mask of the dragon was lowered to reveal a specific playful Fae.

Kai and Mantis were in agreement, "Trick or treat!"

I returned to my feet and stared at them both. "This entire thing was just unintentional? You're gonna get it!"

The ingredients for casting spells were not in my purse, but I didn't require spells to make them suffer. The broom slid into my side when I asked. Kai and Mantis looked at me before turning to flee down different gardens. I chased them down with my broom as weapons. "Come back and you're foolish people! I'll offer you an opportunity to treat yourself for Halloween!

Autumn Harvest

by Virginia M. Barilla

A vibrant orange ribbon is tied my heart.

It is surrounded by the summer's the lush greenness

Unwillingly preparing to leave.

Are you going and warm me for a second day?

Are you able to remember the ways we love playing?

I'll let you forget and meander

In the waterfall's vibrant breathtaking in its stunning colors.

Remember to come back next time,

following the winter's battle the fall's defense.

The time is sown for the new season to blossom,

we will join all of our efforts

When the moon is illuminated by an intense orange glow.

We will do, once the sun is shining

rising up from the top of a hill.

Spring, my dear, you're ready to start with your highly anticipated spill

in the Autumn Harvest

It is just over the next hill.

It's only in Movies

Imagine walking along a dirt path through the park. It's an amazing autumn night. It's chilly at times, however, it's better than harsh winter wind, and the intense summer heat. The air is quiet due to the late hours. The sky is bright red to black ombre with some red.

You're enjoying a great walk, until a sudden squealing sound distracts you out of your mind. A slight swoop and a turn of your head, you look toward the sound, thinking about the source. As you turn your head around, all you can see is the same path that you're taking.

After turning around returning to your original path, you walk however, you speed up your speed. Your mind is running. Scared. Anxious. Was that a noise? Animals? The breeze? Your imagination? Perhaps something other than you?

No. Couldn't be. The kind of stuff that you see is seen in films. It's not happening in reality. Your heart is pounding as you attempt to break the chills that are rushing up your spine.

In order to clear your head, breathe deeply and reduce your speed to a walk. The thoughts are redirected back towards the sky. It's gorgeous outside. The changing colours of the trees appear to line the sky with sparkling lights. The sun never ceases to rise. drops, but soon will disappear with the sky turning dark.

The park's empty is beautiful and beautiful. Picture perfect almost. The bright lights of the gym are reflected by the dim lighting from the streetlights and the dark skyline of trees that are in the background.

A slight rumble makes your heart race. Then you turn around, and see one swing that is swaying little, and making a sound when it swings.

That's odd. There's not a breeze. The air is just as dry as your mouth.

Your pace increases in order to escape the zone as quickly as it is possible. Then, suddenly, a shivering feeling is felt in your chest. It feels as if lung is about to cave into. It becomes more difficult to breathe.

In the corners of your eyes you can make out the movement. You jump. Your shadow is there.

You laugh at yourself for having been so afraid of the smallest thing, you slow down to enjoy the view of the peaceful park usually filled with screaming kids and dogs barking. As you continue walking You swear that you have seen an object move along the forest line from the corner of your eyes However, because of what was previously happening, you do not notice the sight.

The moon is shining over your head. After walking too long and your feet want an afternoon break. While you fight through it, contemplate what's in store for you back at your home. A nice hot shower. After that, you can relax in front of the fire by the fire with a blanket along with homemade cookies. The stomach rumbles over the thought of eating. It's been a while since you've eaten.

In sheer boredom, you decide to count the shattered leaves. One...Two...Three...

There's another sound. This time, however, there's no breeze. It's that distinct sound of the boots banging against the sand. It's like moving. In your direction.

Your mind is racing again, you race at the speed you can. You are able to run further into the woods. You seek shelter from the other. His footsteps that pound are following your.

Try to increase your pace, however the terrain is uneven and fights your efforts. It is difficult to avoid branches that hang low and a few slack roots. Your only concern in your mind is getting to safety. On the opposite side of the forest, is the most crowded street in town. When you reach it and are careful, you'll be secure.

The legs push more vigorously, hoping to get quicker. The lungs expand while you're doing it. These lungs don't have the experience of the pressure of this type. It's not like you often train.

In the middle of nothing, you slip. Sliding down and falling over the flooring. An intense laugh sends chills across your spine. In front of you stands someone you've never encountered before. Holding duct tape.

"No Please! ...""", you cry in desperate hope to reach out to a part of the man who could demonstrate compassion.

The man responds with a deeply heartless laugh. The closer he gets to you, you begin to twirl your body. But, while doing it, a tattered black rag pops up from the blue. It is a moment of trepidation with a numb feeling of this. Your vision gets blurred and you realise, this is the end of your story.

Connection Philip Stephens was a LEGO enthusiast. He would build endlessly, making the most complex models.

He was extremely satisfied with his spaceship. It was an object exquisite that he cherished and placed it on a shelf in front of the bedroom.

He loved playing with his Legos all day long and lay to sleep dreaming about future projects.

Sometimes his family and friends would convince him to get out of the house, along with his Legos and to try out something new. The idea didn't go over well with him However, he loved his family and friends and sometimes, he'd be a little reluctant.

He was pressured to go to a film. It was an exciting movie filled with adventure and action. Phillip was enjoying the film and began to take a break. The time spent with friends was great, he figured. When he stepped to the bowl of popcorn, an unsettling lighting glowed in the theater. Phillip took a deep breath. No! There's no way it could be!

It was.

The huge screen, a bright beam of light filled the sky. It struck a person inside his vehicle and then the driver was taken to a spaceship floating at the top of the skies.

Phillip was able to feel an unwelcome cold sweat appear over his face, and his heart was racing. Phillip's biggest fear was that he would be taken hostage by aliens. Phillip shut his eyes, and pretending to be at back inside his home, constructing his own Lego city in which nothing terrible occurred to any one.

After the film was over, his buddies invited him take a meal out, however, he was tired and longed to return to his home.

In his safe room He pulled out an assortment of Legos and set to work in building a shelter that would block out light from the outside. Making the shelter helped him feel much better after which he became sleepy and ready to retire.

He fell asleep, and then began fantasizing about Lego cities, Lego automobiles, along with Lego boats. He woke up dreaming he was of the tiny Lego pirate figures with an eye patch and an axe in his hands.

Bright light flooded Phillip's bedroom, awakening Phillip from a dream. Phillip woke up to check out what was going on. On top of the bed the bed, his Lego spaceship hovered.

"What the heck?" the man said loudly.

While he was sitting in his chair, a beam light reflected from the Lego spaceship. It traced the path of Phillip's feet toward his head. He's mouth was dry and his heart began to pound inside the chest.

"This can't be happening, I built you," He yelled.

"Thank you, Phillip Stephens," a strange voice replied. "We've searched for a method to contact you and then you offered your number to us. We'd like you to travel with us. We'll be there to pick you up."

"No! I'm not leaving." Phillip scooted up against the wall, slamming his head against the wall just above his bed. This was the place where his spaceship was resting all night.

The spaceship moved closer to the surface while the light beam increased in height close up to the hips.

He'd been scared of alien abductions throughout his life, and it's now occurring. Due to something he'd constructed using Legos. While the idea sank into his head, the bright beam swung towards the top of his chest. The man wasn't certain what could occur if the beam reached the top of his head, but was not willing to know.

He ran across the bed before falling on the ground. He moved to the desk, then reached upwards, grasping the final item he had built. When he snatched it up to your chest, the lights was shattered in the room, and then a loud scream was heard within the back of his head.

In the morning, when the father came knocking on his front door but there was no response. The door was opened and he took a peek into the room. Phillip was not there. His father was scratching his head. Was he there? He spotted a small Lego construction on the floor. He took it and put it on his desk. He was shaking his head.

Phillip was typically more cautious in his Legos.

Inside the small Lego building, Phillip peered out at his father. After his father left of the room Phillip was wrapped over himself, and a tear ran across his cheek.

"I'm sorry, dad," said he muttered. "But I can't let them take me."

10. The Darker Side of Dark: It was an Infant Baby

By Carlos F. Gonzalez

I was blessed enough to be able to have living great-grandparents even as I grew up to the level of a grasshopper. I can remember the warm summer evenings in the south at their adobe ranch in which evenings were filled with stories and an eerie sky. No electric lamps were used around the streets in those days as well, so at night people would sit outside their homes to sip a glass of lemonade, or perhaps a soft drink.

We'd shoot the breeze until the sandman came and made us sleepy Then we'd go to the back of the house. Then we would close our doors as well as windows that were, in fact did not have screen mesh over the windows. Then, we shut them with heavy wooden exterior "shutters." I put these in quotation marks as these were really tiny doors that totally block out any moonlight entering from outside. The inside of the home a creepy, dark feeling. it's a different matter!

At this time my great-grandmother shared with us about her uncle. "I remember a time," she recounted, "when your Uncle Aco was heading home late in the night on his horse. He was at a sale of cattle in the city. He returned home with a number of gold coins packed in the saddle bags. He came to a stop, rolled on a cigar and then ignite it.

"Now, it was a full moon night," she added, "and he could easily observe the entire area. He spotted an unsettling shadow that was visible in the earth that was following him ever as the moon rose. The shadow was not acting as ordinary shadows; it was not influenced by anything in the vicinity, for example, a tree or structures of the rocks, and not even his horse, nor was it casting shadows on the ground around him. The shadow behaved as if you place a bucket of water onto the ground, and it sort of spins around a in the air while extending. It was like it had a personality that was its own.

"But the most bizarre thing he observed was that the day seemed to be more dark than night. It was darker than black. Then it kept pace his movements, first on his left and then ahead of him, and the next time, it was to his right just a couple of metres closer to him. Then it was able to go ahead in the opposite direction and continue to just wait for him to arrive."

She stopped to have one of her lemonades as I contemplated my uncle Aco. He was a man of the streets likely around his mid-80s, slim, tall and as tough like a nut. After having experienced his time during the Mexican Revolution, he'd seen many things which is why he wasn't at all scared.

"Just when he was about to cross the river, the shadow disappeared into the bushes and tall grass. The horse was slowly walking across the smooth river rocks, being careful not to lose its footing, and Aco was smoking his hand-rolled cigar.

They were probably a mere three meters into the river, when he heard it--the sound of a baby crying behind him."

Today, my Uncle Aco (may be with my great-grandmother be at peace) was a kind man. So, I was not surprised to hear that he had pulled his horse off and was turned around. He needed to make certain; this was what kind of man the man was.

"He saw it again and there was definitely crying coming from the direction in which he'd traveled. He led his horse toward the tall grass and bushes and noticed that the shadow which was chasing his horse had vanished. He turned on the carbide lamp, then got off the horse, and began seeking out the reason for the cries. When he began to look at the source, he could feel the anger rising. What could somebody do to abandon a child in the night without anyone around?' he asked.

"The crying was getting more and more louder and he was aware that it was coming closer. It was! In the middle of the long thin grass that was wispy and only a few other things around him lay a child wrapped in a dark grey, rough blanket. The eyes of the boy were red possibly because he had been crying so many times.

"Your Uncle Aco picked him up. "How can your parents let the child here, all alone, with no food, and no someone to look after the child!' He held the little boy within his arms. "Just take a look, very small and tiny... too small. ...'

"A cloud of dark grey-blue clouds suddenly blocked illumination of the moon. The moment in the dark little Aco remarked"I could be small and petite, but just take a look at my teeth and sharp eyes!' The clouds slid away and the moon's glow was shining through the darkness, Aco saw the child clearly. The mouth was packed with very well-developed teeth, extremely blood red hair and eyes that were as brilliant like charcoal embers!

"He abandoned the child and cursed it and then rushed back towards his horse. He ran across the river as swiftly as he could, the child's frightful smile fading when he put more distance between the two. He promised that if he ever had to visit the city in the future and again, he'd remain vigilant, for the event that a new black shadow emerged. He promised to carry Holy Water with him, as well."

I hope that you been entertained by this tale and maybe, you've had as much of the thrill as I got when I first heard about it as a young child.

Chapter 4: Indulgence

A day was especially cold outside. the snow was falling and even with the heating turned on, his mother was shaking. The mother was looking longingly at the blankets that were soft and cozy blankets, however, her son resisted her and pulled his blankets towards him.

Then, at the end of the day, the electricity stopped and the home grew extremely cold, and very frigid.

His mother came to him and begged "Tommy I'm freezing. Do you mind if I lend you one of your luxurious blankets?"

However, Little Tommy Freedom wasn't willing to be a partaker.

"I love you mom, but no," the man told her. "These are MY blankets."

Then, Little Tommy Freedom spontaneously ignited, taking his blankets together with the rest of his blankets.

12. Porch Light

"SWEETIE, I THOUGHT YOU were going to turn the porch light on," George stated at the top of the ladder. He pulled out the Halloween candy bowl off at the rear of the top cabinet, and then slowly moved it back down the steps.

"I did turn it on," Tanya phoned back in the bathroom.

"I can see it from here, and it's not on," the man said using a dish towel to clean the dust that was in the bowl.

"Well, maybe it burned out," she said her back.

"We won't get any trick-or-treaters without the porch light!" He put the bowl down before grabbing the bulb he had saved from the drawer. "Never mind, I'll get it."

George took the stepladder, and then opened the door to the front. The aroma of roasted pumpkins was immediately awaited him at two of the jack-o'-lanterns that were on the porch. He lowered the stepladder and then climbed it. He reached out to pull out the old bulb, the light shook in the palm of his hand. "That's strange." ..." The bulb is not working," he said. He was able to tighten the bulb and it shined brilliantly. He shook his head and was able to open the door. "It was just loose!" He said. Then He turned around to grab the ladder.

A person was on the sidewalk just in front of the ring of light created by the porch light. "Oh, geez!" the man said standing up with his heart beating. The size of the shoes was too large to fit the body, and the baggy pants were ripped at the knees, the shirt that was not tied on the other side, and the sleeves sloppily. The face of the child was drenched in shadows.

"You have scared me", child. Return in a couple of moments and we'll be there to greet your return." He climbed up the ladder. "Tell all your acquaintances that they're getting Dagbars! The biggest ones." And then the man went into his room. "Are you prepared sweetie? It's time for the kids to appear!" He put the bulb in the drawer before putting the stepladder on the counter.

"One second, almost done."

George broke open the container of Dagbars and put them in the bowl. "Alright. I'm going to put the candy near at the front door." When he stepped from the kitchen, Tanya stood there wearing her skull-themed catsuit in makeup.

"Boo," she said.

"Fantastic. It's all I need is to make my ..." I'm not sure." He glared at her.

"What's wrong?" she demanded.

"The porch light is off again."

He turned around and headed towards the front door, turning the switch off and on frequently. "I don't understand," He said. But then the boy was walking along the sidewalk with his back against the streetlamp in the road. Did he alter the lamp?

George was looking upwards at the lamp, it was still on top of the porch. It was impossible for the child could have climbed the light. "Sweetie, grab the stepladder, will you?" He asked, while keeping watch on the little one sitting motionless in the yard. The kid didn't even move in the breeze, however the mellow wind of autumn threw his hair up. Tanya was also there, along as well, accompanied by the stepladder.

"Thanks, honey. This kid has been in the middle of the night. This isn't just me, is it? That's creepy, right?"

"I guess so," she commented, looking at the dark. "It is Halloween though."

"Hmm," George said, going outside again. He got up the ladder and inspected the bulb. The bulb was still loose and the bulb was tightened and was on. He moved it around to make sure that it really was there And, satisfied and climbed up. The child had not moved.

An accidental splash called eye to a dark pool close to the child's left foot. A dark, thin line appeared from the cuff, moved across the wrist until its finger, then expanded to form a second splash. "You okay, kid? Are you injured?" he asked. The child did not respond. He didn't move a muscle.

In complete silence, George climbed down, made a turn, then said across his shoulder. "Grab me a Dagbar, will you?" George offered a hand and Tanya dropped the candy bar.

"Here, kid. Trick or Treat." He dropped the candy bar and the child did nothing to grab the candy bar. It landed on his chest.

"George!" Tanya said however she did not follow-up when the Dagbar was thrown to the pavement right in front of her child. The child remained in the sand with the bar on his foot. George took the ladder in and shut the door with a wide-eyed smile. "Creeeeeepy!" she said with a tune. Both laughed uncontrollably as they dragged the gooseflesh off from their arms.

"I'm going to get my mask. I'll let you know if he eats some sweets." He ran through the hallway to their bedroom. He stopped short after she shouted "George!" He turned and went back.

"What's the matter?"

"The light went out again!"

"Did the kid do it?"

"I don't know! I don't think he's on the other side of the street. I glanced away for a second!"

George turned his attention to the outside and saw that the streetlamp was on too. "Grab the flashlight." He grabbed the ladder, then opened the door with a gap and looked out into the dark. He was unable to see beyond the front porch and the porch, but he'd solve the problem.

"Here you go," she told him, before and handed him a flashlight. He set up the ladder on the porch, then climbed two steps, and reached upwards towards the malfunctioning bulb as he turned his flashlight. Tanya screamed.

The boy was still at exactly the same place. The flashlight's beam was shining on his face. A portion of his face was broken, with the skin was ripped away.

Bone fragments protruded from the sunken pile. The little one whipped the arm that was bleeding to shield its eyes from the sun.

George dropped off the ladder, and he sped to the home. Tanya shut the door. The two fled through the family room before returning towards the kitchen.

"What was that?" Tanya exclaimed.

"I don't know!" George shouted while panting. He snatched the phone from the wall's the cradle.

"Who are you calling?"

"I don't know! Police?"

The lights of the family room flickered out.

Seeing Double

IRIS and her father were among the numerous father-daughter pairs who dressed up in the roles of Captain Galaxy and Galaxy Girl in their community. Six-year-old IRIS walked around and frolicked in the sparkling purple skirt that hung around her waist. The mask of purple, strapped by an elastic band, was a bit uncomfortable however it was well worth the discomfort.

The girl looked at her father who was dressed as superhero, Captain Galaxy. The tears had to be shed in order to convince him to wear the costume to go Halloween. The effort was worthwhile.

"Daddy, do you think the real Captain Galaxy and Galaxy Girl are out here trick or treating too?"

"I doubt it, dear. It seems like they're surrounded by plenty of bad guys to combat to be worried about trick-or-treat."

"But is it possible that a criminal person was trying to track them? Isn't it better to cover up in places in a place where there are many individuals dressed in the same way and no one would be able to discern them?"

Her father smiled. "Well, in that case, I suppose it would."

The group stopped at an apartment with a nighttime blue and purple dragon as well as a scary knight who was guarding his garden. Iris took a walk and handed the candy from a huge shimmering bowl.

"I am in love with your outfit. Galaxy Girl is my favorite," said the princess while she threw an ample amount of her bag.

"Thank you," Iris told her. She turned around and ran towards her dad. As they were about to leave, Iris heard a familiar voice calling her name.

"Iris is that you?" was the question asked by an older girl approximately 14 years old dressed in Galaxy Girl.

"Wow, your costume is so good, you could be the real Galaxy Girl." Iris declared while running towards the girl.

"Ah, thank you, I made it myself." She rubbed her purple face "I bet you don't know who I am?"

"I do, too," declared Iris. "Daddy I'm Hannah. Hannah is a dancer at my school and is a helper with my classes. She's amazing."

"Oh damn, my name has been revealed. Did you even know it was Iris?"

"Your voice, silly." Iris handed her silver and purple gift bag. "See how much candy I got?"

"Oh you're right it's quite a bit. What are you planning to do? take it all in?"

"Very slowly," said her father.

"Where's your candy, Hannah?"

"I uh, lost it. My dad actually was looking for it. I'm waiting to see if he will be back."

"Oh it's so tragic. You can have my candy together."

"You aren't required to do it, Iris. It's just fine. Oh look, here comes my dad now."

A man of a tall build who had a huge chest, walked at them, wearing a authentic appearance Captain Galaxy costume. The costume was dark purple and midnight blue spandex with spirals of galaxy that resembled an enlarged G across the chest of his. His face was concealed by a mask made with midnight blue.

"Any sign of it?" she demanded before he was able to say anything.

"No," he replied. After that, almost in satisfaction, he added, "I think we've lost it for good."

"No that's awful!" shouted Iris. "I'll bring some candy to class for you."

"Oh, thank you Iris, you're so sweet." Hannah was able to reach out and brushed her hair.

Hannah's dad removed his throat. "We really should get going."

Then, out of the bush came a metal beast. It stood about 2 feet tall, and it was armed with three cameras in the front of the body. The legs of four spiders grew from the sides of its body and ended up in a pair of pincher feet. three claws attached to each of these.

"Located Captain Galaxy," it said, in a voice that was synthesized. After that, it read "Located Galaxy Girl."

"Ahhh," said Iris, "that's so cool."

The machine turned to stare at her. "Located Galaxy Girl."

Iris tried to hold her hand. "No, honey," told her father while pushing her back. "You might break it."

"Located Captain Galaxy," The machine said. It tilted its head in a gaze back towards Hannah as well as her father. "Located Captain Galaxy and Galaxy Girl." It was looking at Iris as well as her father. Then it became distracted as it walked past another Captain Galaxy and Galaxy

Girl passed by. "Captain Galaxy?" it demanded. Static was growing in its voice. "Must destroy Captain Galaxy."

Another collection of superheroes was spotted. It was in my opinion the most original. The male wore a violet duster with an evening blue suit, and the lady wore a violet dress that was paired with a midnight blue corset. Both were wearing goggles to cover their heads.

"Steampunk Captain Galaxy?" asked Hannah's dad.

"You know it!" The stranger replied by waving.

"Nice Job."

"Thanks, yours isn't bad either."

The machine accompanied the steampunk couple with its eyes when they left. "Captain Gal . . . Gal. Not Gal.

Not Captain Galaxy. But not Galaxy Girl." It was back to Iris as well as her father. "Captain Galaxy located."

Hannah's dad yelled out "I'm the real Captain Galaxy, can't you tell?"

The machine spun. "Captain Galaxy located."

Iris stood up and tapped her feet. "No, my daddy is Captain Galaxy."

The robot once more was able to turn around. "Captain Galaxy? Where is it?" It started spinning on its own. It began to smell when its processors became overwhelmed.

"Look, Captain Galaxy is using his gravity powers to increase his mass!" Hannah exclaimed, then directed her attention to the inflatable dragon. The robot halted and aimed at the dragon.

"CAPTAIN GALAXY LOCATED," it read. A bizarre looking spike emerged from the side, right below the lenses that it uses to see. It swung the dragon around and pierced it with an explosive sound.

When the princess got on her lawn to inspect the dragon, an explosion rattled all around the area as the robotic began to self-destruct. Her father was hunched over the princess to keep her safe from the blast. When the sound in her ears gradually diminished, Iris peeked out to see the destruction. The princess lay in the dirt and her arms were covering her head. While Iris was watching the princess slowly rise and appeared to be in good spirits.

The yard contained tiny crater that was that was where the inflatable dragon used be and where the Scarecrow Knight was on fire. The yard was empty of Hannah or her father.

Mr. Roboto? Maybe it was created in the lab of Professor Proton." Hannah sat on the ground, and raked out the tiny metallic pieces--all which was left from the robot seeking.

"I think it's getting late and we should probably go back and check on your mom."

Hannah stood up. "Oh Do you think Hannah will be angry over the dragon? The dragon really enticed her."

Captain Galaxy held her hand over her shoulder. "She's just going to be glad you're all right."

"Dad Did we have the right idea? Are you hiding in the dark as we did? Iris may have been hurt."

"Hannah Sometimes heroes need to take tough decisions to for instance . . . A carefully calculated chance. It's also me that instructed you to return home." He wrapped the girl in a tense hug. "You did a great job distracting the robot."

"Thanks dad. Are you sure we should still be trick-or-treating?"

He turned his head. "I thought you were too old?"

"Well there's a reason why every girl out there would like to be me even if it was only for a single night. Tonight is, however, the sole night that I am able to fully be me. I am both of me."

Chapter 5: Clear Of The Cemetery

The STORM CLOUDS swept across the grey sky. I was shaken as the lights was visible on the horizon, signaling the impending storm.

"What is it you're waiting for? You can do it. Or...are you an animal?" Pierre laughed as we walked by the gate of Louisiana's famous Saint Louis Cemetery Number One. He slack-mindedly adjusted his watch and it radiated an iridescent green glow which displayed the date: eleven fifty-five p.m.

I swallowed hard and felt my heart started to beat quicker, but I smiled at my companion and I said "Are you serious? I'd repeat this routine every single day and two times on a Saturday." I reached inside my bag and grabbed my flashlight. "Come on. Let's get this done."

I made up a brave face and opened the old gates.

The hinges shouted and moan when the gate opened. The noise echoed through the mausoleums as if trying to awaken the dead. I pointed my flashlight directly in the direction of the sun, but the fog had begun to roll into. The fog was so thick that I was unable to see my feet while we moved forward through the darkness.

"Now I wonder, where's that ancient witch's tomb? There's nothing to see within this mist!" Pierre was referring to Marie Laveau, a long defunct voodoo witch. Like a stern warning to her burial place and slept, thunder began to roar. An abrupt gust of wind floated around the tombs. It could have could be a sound of wailing. Lightning flashes showed a concrete building in the distance, and the fog was swaying all around the structure. The fog sprang up but then backed away in a way as if inviting us to move forward.

"Pierre, it's right there--just ahead." The man was quiet, and I surveyed the area, but I could not see him because of the dark fog. I could feel his breath as well as the faint sound of footsteps to my side told that my friend was in the area.

A sudden whiff of decay was aplenty in my nostrils and I felt like a dead animal that was cooked under the scorching sunshine for a few days. While we were walking towards the burial crypt, an eerie bloody smell of copper was evident throughout the air.

"Do you smell that?" I inquired. I looked to direction to see his footsteps however I only heard an ominous sound in response. It sounded to me like a snort of nausea which is why I laughed at myself, and said "Weak wuss." A handful of more steps, before we stood just in front of Marie's crypt.

"Well, here we are," I said by a small breath. The crypt was lined with crosses and an X. Little trinkets were hanging in the corners, and dying flowers everywhere. "Alright, Pierre. Let's go about this. If we can go faster to sleep, the earlier the morning will arrive and we'll finish and head home."

I delved into my backpack to get my blanket that I laid over the ground just near the graveyard. The smell of decayed flesh was more intense than it had ever been, however I attributed it to the fact that I was in an old cemetery. I never imagined it would be smelling like a florist shop. I lay in my couch and tried to be at ease on the hard cold surface.

"Might as well spread out your blanket and get comfortable too," I said when I laid back. I didn't hear a word from Pierre however I could hear footsteps from the distant distance. I laughed at myself.

"Oh, Pierre! What's that chicken doing?" I stretched out on my bed, shut my eyes, and tried to fall asleep, hoping that the morning was coming soon.

Because Pierre left and left, nobody would be any wiser had I gone also, however I've not been the type of person to back to a challenge. I'm not sure why I got there, but it was being a slumbering victim in that muddy, misty cemetery.

I felt the warmth of the sun's warmth over my face and realized it was the morning. I opened my eyes, and I was ready to fold over as I saw the scene. In front of the crypt was a splash of deep crimson, shiny and sparkling with the dawn sun. I squealed and could feel the warm air slide over my tongue. It also twitched my nostrils. It was a taste. I could taste blood that was in the air.

I inspected the stain in crimson and noticed tiny, feminine footprints which led me back towards the burial chamber. Small blood-red footprints were spotted on the edges of the seal made from cement that sealed Marie Laveau's remains in.

"What happened here while I slept?" I murmured. "Pierre is going to freak out when I tell him about this." I began to get away after hearing the sounds of the cracks and crumbling. I turned to find the crypt was crumbling and concrete fragments as well as dust sat in a heap under the inscribed. The overwhelming smell of decay was once more in the air.

The opening was in the middle, between the rocks that had been hacked up, there was a pale, nearly grey, hand. The fingers were damaged and bloody it was as if someone was gnawing at the floor while being dragged into the inside. When I looked closely, I saw the flash of green light across the wrist of the deceased. Pierre's watch!

"Oh my God!" I shouted. "Oh the Lord! Pierre!"

I was shocked as the hand vanished out of the view, and slipped further down the tomb. A soft, gravelly laugh was heard from the tomb. I backed off slowly, and after which I slipped on a marker for the foot. While I struggled to stand in the mud, a slender, dark face appeared inside the broken graveyard. The lips were curled between yellow and rotten teeth. I heard a horrible, low voice shouting at me.

The Halloween Quilt

The River cut across the mountains and gave boats to towns further away and varied work opportunities to people living in Riverton. Although the town was tiny however, it was the largest community, looking at each other. On holidays, they would often celebrate as one large family. Visitors to town seeking a home to call home, were never in a state of isolation for very lengthy. They easily became part of the local community, and were accepted for their individuality, nothing more and or less.

Ian Michaels was just this kind of transfer. Ian was a newcomer to town, and got a job at the school's elementary as the school's Janitor. He was an older, single male with no children that he could call his own. The community was an ideal match for him. He loved keeping the school neat and watching kids as they went through the hall between classes, or playing in the playground. The school was his home for a long time and was a great help.

If school closed during the summer months however, that didn't mean the teacher was no longer working. work because there were constant repairs needed to be made and projects that did not disrupt education of the students. In addition, it was an opportunity for community groups could make use of the space to finish projects that would have been done easily at a business location or even in a person's house.

It was during the summer of this year that Riverton Quilt Guild Riverton Quilt Guild decided they were going to make a huge Halloween-themed quilt that would be displayed in the library of the school. It was displayed just behind the chair of the librarian within the reading circle that was carpeted part in the library. Every week, youngsters would go to the library to read for an hour. They sat on the floor in front of the library and screen and read the story. After that, they could explore the library and pick books they could bring to home.

The town's ladies have, through the years produced a number of special occasion or seasonal quilts that could be displayed on the wall. In the spring meeting of quilters, it was agreed the quilt for Halloween should be quilted and pieced during the course of summer. The women designed and developed the quilt. They picked a variety of blocks for the quilt to create. They would piece them with geometric shapes that could be stitched together with a sewing machine, and certain blocks would be appliqued with a simpler stitching with a hand. The group chose a black cat and a spider. They also picked spider webs, witches with an eerie black cauldron, Jack-o'-Lanterns and tombstones with engraved R.I.P., a skeleton and ghost.

The summer progressed and the quilt was assembled The ladies decided that when some were hand-quilting around the frame for their quilts while others took turns reading out loud Halloween stories. The stories could be humorous, but others were frightening and terrifying. As they hung out the stories' words stories were accidentally transferred to the quilt stitch for stitch.

The quilt was completed at the right time for it for it to go up in the hallway on Halloween morning. Children paraded around the halls wearing costumes, and then went to the library for a story time. The children were happy and eager to return home for Trick-or-Treat in their neighborhood. It was an enjoyable experience to go out until late and collect candy. These are two events that are rarely seen.

After school the following day the librarian noticed that the chairs and plants were turned upside down. There was even dead mice in close proximity to the circulation desk.

The school's office was contacted to request that Ian arrive and help set the situation in order, but Ian did not show up to work, and nobody was able to contact Ian. The entire town was puzzled. What was the matter with Ian? What happened to him? Police and townspeople were looking for him, but he'd gone missing.

As the janitor was not identified, the school sought out an agency that could provide temporary work and then employed a temporary worker to take over until Ian was back. The employee from the agency worked for several days. However, the next day, he wasn't located the school realized that they'd have to find the new cleaner.

Harry Sell was eventually hired to become a popular part of the local community. As Ian He loved seeing the smiling children at the entrance and in the playground, and also kept the structure in good condition.

In mid-October the following year, the quilt for Halloween was hung on the display walls at the right time to celebrate the celebration. The day before

Halloween, the kids participated in a school parade, as well as the librarian gave stories in story hour.

Miss Courtney's students came to the library to have their turn, and the librarian was reading "The Library Mouse of Back Creek Glen." When she told the tale of the mouse's eyes, those on the cat's face in the quilt lit up. Small Amy Darling interrupted the librarian in the course of reading and pointed out the quilt. She asked "Why do the cat's eyes light up?" The librarian explained to Amy that it was sunlight from the windows which makes it appear that way and continued the story.

After a few minutes the librarian, After a while, Miss Courtney quit the library in order to make a short errand for the offices. The little Amy Darling once again interrupted the librarian and pointed to the quilt and asking "Why did the Jack-o-lantern look at the door when Miss Courtney left?"

The librarian said, "It's an optical illusion. It happens that when we are looking at patterns, our eyes change the images we see due to the black material against the orange. Therefore, it is possible to think that it moved but in reality, it wasn't." The rest of the story time went on as normal and the students returned back to their room.

The kids were elated throughout the day Their emotions were amplified due to the sugary drinks they had at parties. Then, at the end of the day, they boarded their busses and headed for home. They were dreaming of chocolate and sweets inside their heads, and looked forward to playing outside in the evening dressed in costumes.

Harry was asked to clean up his school. There was a lot of garbage and drinking drinks that had spilled within the classes. The floors had to be cleaned. The day was more long than normal, and when it was over it, the sun was already been set. While he was walking by at the library was greeted by an animal meow.

It can't be true an excuse, he pondered. Was there someone who left a window unlocked and let a cat inside? The library's door was pushed open using one hand while his hand reached towards the light switch in order that the cat could check. Prior to turning his switch Harry had to be pushed back into the space while the door shut in front of him.

As he walked from the hallway that was brightly lit to the dim library Harry became temporarily blind and lost. His heart was racing while his eyes slowly shifted. With the light of the moon shining through the windows, he could observe the library as a chaos. He sat in a tense position and was stunned looking at the space.

Spider webs were everywhere as well as eyes that were blinking. An unrelenting rumbling sound was heard in the direction of the workroom in the library and the sounds of water running. A cat suddenly jumped into his path in a way that frightened him.

There was a cackle, and the lights in the office stunk and created a tiny swath of lighting over the library. A woman's sinister voice spoke, "We've been waiting patiently for you."

"Who's there and what are you doing in here?" He yelled out while his way to the office. "You've made a mess of the entire library!"

"Get him," the voice called out.

Harry had a second time heard the sound of rattling and was able to feel a gentle tapping sound across his shoulders. When he began to move around, a ghost swooped at the back of his head, causing him to stumble. The cat charged at him and sunk the claws of its feline friends into his legs, causing him to fall back farther.

He was wedged between two shelves. He was frantically waving his arms in an attempt to lift himself from the webbing which lay over all surfaces. In the midst of his panic and thought about it, his mind raced. Why is this happening? What can I do to escape?

While he struggled and struggle, the eyes that the man had seen earlier grew closer and, to his horror they were eyes of a massive spider. The spider swiftly twisted the injured Harry into a tightly encased cocoon and he was unable to move the same time as if he were being paralyzed. The tiny gap between the webbing would allow Harry to observe what was happening and was a bit frightening.

The sound of the water was abruptly quiet, and in the bright light of the kitchen, Harry saw a big black cauldron that was balanced on a broomstick and floating in the air. In the background of the cauldron stood a sexy witch, with covered in warts and a pocked nose. By swiping the witch's fingers the cauldron was placed upon the floor at the front to the library.

There was a cat scurrying in the library. After he killed and pounced on one of the mice The witch instructed him to place the corpse in its "usual" place.

"Check out the books? No, I don't think so! Look at the mouse!" she said with delight.

"Gather around boys," she ordered. The ghost, skeleton cat and spider were gathered in the pot. "This is our evening and we're planning to enjoy it to the fullest. We've been waiting a year to enjoy these couple of minutes. In the past, we've been gypped off of enjoying ourselves. It was impossible to glance through the area, look at possible options and make plans, as the quilt was put up to the wall on the morning of our very special day. After that, the fun of last year suffered an attack on the heart.

"This time we're going to develop a style because we know whatever goes in the cauldron stays in the cauldron." The witch shook her head in a long, hard cackle. "Those small morsels of food which came in to listen to the ramblings of this librarian would've been fun to play with, but were all gone before the darkness. It's a shame. The girl filled them with all of that rainbow and sunshine. The lessons we could have given them were more. They could have been educated," she sneered.

The attention of the witch turned to Harry. The witch pointed him in the direction of Harry and inquired, "Do you boys remember what he told me after he saw me in the quilt? He told me I was "scary ugly'. Would you say that it was appropriate to be saying? No! The boys are now ready to let start the fun." Harry flinched in shock at what appeared to be the imminent demise of his friend. The players "played" for hours.

At dawn, the witch said "until next year boys," and the boys returned to their respective places upon the quilt. The library's webbing was gone and there was no proof about their existence, or Harry's were found.

As the school day began and the librarian was in the library for her first day. The librarian stopped abruptly at the entrance and stared in horror at the chairs that had fallen over and the plants. Then she noticed something at the desk for circulation and, slowly her way towards the desk. It was the mouse.

Her thoughts whirred back to the events of the previous year. She gasped for air as she attempted to settle her heart racing. In a frenzied manner, she took a walk to her phone at the desk, and rang the office of the school.

"Would you be able to request Harry to stop by the library? I'm in need of help with to clean up my messy mess."

"Harry isn't here. We're trying to contact the person, but he's not responding to his call," the secretary responded.

Chapter 6: The Haunted Canal Town

METAMORA is a town that doesn't have an intersection or stoplight. There are a few hundred residents in the village without a incorporated entity which doubles in size as visitors arrive on weekend. Tourists come to view the sole working wooden aqueduct that exists throughout the United States.

The canal runs throughout the Hamlet. The only stop-signal reminds people to be mindful prior to crossing the bridge, and tracks for trains. During warmer seasons, trains travel across in the Whitewater Valley to bring additional tourists to shops, canal-boat excursions, and historical education.

Every day the county sheriff deputy walks through the town in order to ensure the peaceful. There isn't a great deal of police are needed in Metamora.

One of the main complaints is the volume at which the whistle of the train blares in after-hours naps. Most disagreements are resolved how they have been for two centuries--privately. It is not necessary to contact the sheriff when you're fighting your relatives.

Weekend tourists are an uninhabited town. The town's residents tell tales of the canal's first boat packed with politicians, that sank five feet in the muddy water, as the town's only scandal. The city's past is littered with accounts of drownings, murders as well as shootings, arsenic poisonings banks, explosions, bank robberies and train wrecks. There are also ill-fated love triangles and failed jumping across canal locks.

The past's decadence becomes alive during the late at night. If it's quiet, the spirits awake and adds to the Metamora dark. The white woman is taken on a nighttime walk along the town's gazebo. The ghostly silhouette of a tiny child glistens the window of the tavern in which they are now. From a distant source, the whistled songs of an earlier period fill the atmosphere with crickets.

There is a legend that says the Colliers resided in Metamora during the first half of 1800. John Collier lived on a farm along with his wife. Indiana had experienced a massive increase and its residents could make money through determination. The Colliers took down the massive hickory over their property to meet the wood requirements of the territory which was recently granted Statehood. John did his best to make sure he had enough his family with food and shelter.

John Collier had an unmarried brother who lived with his sister on the top of the hill. Wilbur Collier lived through the generosity of his sister and brother. The man viewed job as a sign of an allergy and should be kept away from. Most people viewed him of the town's inhabitants as a laidabout and a whirlwinder who would often be heard to whistle at his idleness. The man was frequently wandering and uninhibitedly whistles across the railway tracks, without a specific destination in mind.

A few days ago, Wilbur did not return the mule he borrowed when he was expected to return. Looking to end the argument like brothers, Wilbur swung at John but missed striking his mother-in-law. John became angry and swung at Wilbur shouting, "No one hits my wife!"

Following a brief fight, John overpowered Wilbur and put his brother on the floor. "Hit him!" he shouted at his wife. Thwack! Wilbur was struck unconscious by a Hickory stick.

John did not stop teaching his younger brother lessons. He resorted to expressing his frustration by delivering blows after blow on Wilbur's chest and head. "You are lazy!" Slam! "You are good for nothin'!" Pop! "I want you gone!" Then gurgle! Then, Wilbur met his eternal rest by striking him with one last strike. "Stop whistling!" Thud!

Wilbur was laid to rest at the farm of his family. John wasn't charged with the murder. The incident was one of family disputes at the time. John as well as his wife and their children remained in Metamora and contributed to the building of Metamora to become a canal-based town.

It was Wilbur who has left the most significant legacy to those Colliers who resided in Metamora. It's the sound of Wilbur's whistling which continues to play unsettling tones despite his brother's final request. Metamora's spirit walk with a rhythm, to whatever music Wilbur whistles while he goes on his walk along the railway tracks.

"The MasterChef Mouse", MEREDITH COOPER was scurried about, taking the dogs out, and the cats inside, and putting out food as well as a bowl of cream to the cats. The bird feeders were checked and then sprayed the plants with water. It was early in the morning but she wanted to be sure that everything was taken care of before her husband was due to come home for breakfast.

He brewed his cup of coffee, and put the table in order for one. The woman walked quietly out the driveway, and picked up the paper from the day's newspaper. She removed it from its wrapper, folded it and placed it on his napkin on the table. She checked everything.

It seemed like she was completed, perfect and flawless, until she realizing that she had to take out the garbage in the kitchen and place it into a new garbage bag. The man didn't like to be able to smell anything coming out of the garbage bin in the kitchen even though she was cautious about it, or at least she believed.

To be prepared it was necessary, she walked out and picked a couple of flowers from her flower garden and placed them in the jar of a tiny canning container that she placed on the table. It was her fear that the man might think it to be overly feminine or a bit over-the-top and unnecessary. She was trying to figure out what she wanted the best option when she heard him banging through the steps.

Her heart rate picked up. The bacon was ready while his bread was on the toaster. Her coffee was ready when the man sat down. The coffee was as black, which means there was no requirement for cream, milk or sugar. He carefully turned the bacon over and carefully so that she did not spill it out. After it was cooked and set, she placed it on a towel to let it drain and then crisp up little. Then she cracked two eggs in the bacon grease exactly as he likes they were, and then put the toast in the toaster. It was a blessing that she put out the butter that night prior to. He didn't like hard, brittle sticks of butter.

He sipped the coffee, and looked at him with a grimace - it was very hot. Perhaps, it was it was too hot. It would have been better to pour it as soon as she heard his voice so that it allowed time to cool slightly. Well, next time. She'd learn.

He flipped the paper open then shook it up then folded it in a proper manner and started reading. The woman walked from one place to the other between egg fryers as well as the toaster. He was happy with his eggs perfectly cooked, with the whites perfectly done and yolks cooked to perfection. He waited patiently for that moment and carefully placed eggs on the plate followed by salting and peppering them.

She pulled the toast out and coated each piece with butter. She cut toast across the diagonal way, which is what her preference, then put bacon and eggs in a frame with triangular pieces. Perfect. The lady wished that she had fresh parsley on the table to serve with it However she'd surely be seen as over the top.

He shook his head when she threw a jolt on his arm when she placed the dish in front of him. The woman wondered if she had an easier way of doing this. It's possible, she thought. He ripped the paper in half and turned it over, unfolding it and then reading the current latest news.

The dishwashing lady was quiet as she cleaned the dishes and then led the cats to their respective areas until they got beneath his feet. They ended by kicking them out the front door. She brought food to the animals outside. She cleaned the stovetop and polished it up into a shiny finish and cleaned out the sink when she'd do the same thing within a couple of minutes after the dog had finished his meal.

She squinted at her husband. He had snatched the toast piece and began to eat the toast. This must have awakened his appetite because he set the newspaper on top of his plate, as he, still reading consumed the bacon and eggs. He sip his coffee, and at the end of his drink then he put the cup empty toward her while continuing to read. It was a sign to "fill it," so she filled it up. Then he sipped the beverage while doing his reading. He picked up the empty plates and other utensils then cleaned them before wiping out the sink.

In that instant she was grateful she didn't have kids. She was not sure she would be able to cope with the extra tasks. It was impossible to even think of what the process would be like to do, and even what he'd have to do if he were forced to stand in line while she took care for the kids. She turned her head to get rid of the thoughts.

Meredith was still a young woman. Her age was 27 and her husband Larry was just 35. Larry was an accountant who worked hard who had a calendar to follow. There was a calendar too, one that he had drawn up for her. In the beginning, he'd figured out that she was unsure of what to do with him. He wrote an outline of the chart. She was required to checkmark next to each thing after she had completed it. The couple had been together for 4 years, and she'd learned the list, not having to study it and mark items off.

He was finished with his paper. This meant that it was the right time to grab his jacket, suit and briefcase and set up at the door of the house, which she did. He handed her his coat first and then his briefcase. He brushed her cheek before saying goodbye and telling her to put dinner served before 6:30pm. She assured him that she would. and he walked out of the door.

She drew a deep breath. Through the windows, she observed him pull the vehicle out of the driveway, and then pull away. After he had left her view, she settled on the sofa, and laid on the couch for a while. It was a long time since she had slept. To be able to finish everything she needed to wake up earlier than her husband so that she could wash clean her hair, put on makeup, then dress and get dressed in silence and at night so as to not distract the other. After that, she needed to head downstairs, to the kitchen and start breakfast. This was a routine however, it was instilled into her for such a long time that she'd become accustomed to it.

Meredith was the middle-sister of three sisters. She was the unnoticed student of boring college professors who loved to stay all night in the library, smoking and drinking with their dull friends. Girls were required to remain at home and out of view, not the fact that Meredith did ever feel she was even in their view. Meredith was the mouse in the household.

Her elder sister was beautiful, tall and intelligent, she had numerous lovers. She picked out the wealthiest and most attractive one to get married. Their little sister was small and slender, similar to their mom, but as well, intelligent. As she was their younger sister, the older one was a fan of playing with her like dolls, before she arrived.

Meredith smiled. Her mind was a bit shaky. dreaming about her day and start working in order to make all things in order prior to his arrival back home. The house was cleaning, the dinner preparations to cook and laundry to be done, dogs to bathe, and a yard that needed water to look great. Therefore, she took on a lot of work.

After that, she straightened her up and filed the newspaper into his office as the way he liked it. The paper had to be like normal. She then put the sprinklers of water on the lawn. She then bathed their dogs and dried them off and scrubbed them clean. Perfect. It's time to clean the house and sweep furniture. They cleaned bathrooms and polished mirrors. The windows were spot-sprayed.

The chef went into the kitchen to prepare an unusual tiramisu. It was the first time she'd ever made it however, she did have the recipe. There was only one essential ingredient, and she'd purchased just enough. She gently whipped the cream before adding the espresso powder, as well as ladyfingers that were soaked in rum. Then she added her unique ingredient that is guaranteed to make it taste more delicious. When all the layers were finished the cake was placed in the fridge. It's a good gift for someone else, she thought.

The woman turned her attention to the dinner. The previous evening, she had taken a delicious tenderloin of beef to freeze. The time was right to sprinkle it with seasoning and prepare it for baking. The cook cut some onions and peeled carrots and potatoes to serve with the roast. She put the roast as well as the vegetables in the oven. Then she made rolls, too. However, she would not put them into the oven until after 6:15 to ensure they'd be cooked in time.

They set up the table using the most elegant linens. She placed chargers underneath their most elegant plates. They set out an wine glass to him as she wasn't much at all a drinker. She cut some flowers to dress the table, and then she lit two ivory tapers.

He heard the car pulling towards the garage. The rolls were quickly placed in the oven, and then removed her apron. While waiting for him to arrive, she considered, this would look nice.

He opened the door to the foyer and looked around while she stood in front of the kitchen area, waiting for his approval. He smiled at her and handed her his briefcase, then took off his jacket.

The briefcase was set down and put his jacket back inside the hall closet. She took the briefcase to the office, and then came back and found him sitting in the living room, drinking himself a small glass of brandy.

"When is dinner going to be ready?"

"In approximately five minutes. It took me a bit longer in putting the bread into the oven. I hope you're enjoying this aroma, however."

"I'd enjoy tasting them more, you know," the man said, looking at his wristwatch.

"Yes, dear. I prepared special treats for you this evening. I'm sure you'll love the dessert." The girl smiled.

The alarm went off the timer in the kitchen and the cook pulled the dinner from the oven. They set food bowls on the table. They were seated in silence.

When they had finished their main course, she wiped the plates, and set them by the sink. they would wash them in the future.

The tiramisu was pulled out of the fridge. It was beautiful, with freshly chocolate shavings dipped in of the cream. The girl showed him the picture with pride.

"Yes I do, and it's gorgeous. Could I try it?" She cut a huge slice for him, as well as a smaller one for her. She watched him the man eat the food.

He nodded. "This is good," the man declared. Then he ate it.

"Would you like a second slice?" she inquired.

"Yes." She watched when he was eating the next piece. The coffee cup was refilled when he threw the cup in his hands, after which she took their plates and started washing dishes. She didn't turn back. She ate the dishes and also the cookware and pots. She wasn't in a hurry at all, which is why she sat back and enjoyed her meal.

It was a peaceful and tranquil space in the kitchen. So serene and peaceful, with no needs. After she washed the sink, she wiped it clean before slowly turning around.

The head of his was sunk across the table. The cheeks and lips were flaring. His tongue was blue and swelling, sticking from his mouth and between the teeth. His eyes were awestruck and wide, but not blinking.

She sat back, and smiled at her. She knew that it was an allergy to the peanut paste she had added to her tiramisu. It had been long gone, tossed away alongside the rubbish which had been swept away in the morning.

Chapter 7: The Musicians As Well As The Werewolves

At one point In the kingdom of Saloreval it was home to an ensemble of musicians, known in the form of the Saloreval Hieskul Band. Out of all the musicians who played in Saloreval that they played, they were among the most well-known and experienced. They were so proficient in their playing that they enjoyed the adulation of the King Jokkil and were able to perform at any official functions of the monarchy, like the sports competitions, that were the King's preferred divert, along with any state procession. This is why they earned an excellent reputation to maintain and were able to practice each day for hours without a break.

They Saloreval Hieskul Band had a key to their popularity - in addition to being adept at playing their instruments they also had a thorough understanding of the art of magic. The band members had not taken part in any of the high Schools of Wizardry, which existed throughout the Kingdom, as most likely, their previous teachers or classmates might have been able to recognize the mages as skilled However, certain of them were educated by noble parents with the means to pay for individual (and secret) instruction, and handed their wisdom on to people around them. The combination of the two art forms created amazing music that was appealing to everyone who heard it. However, because magic was thought to be too exquisite to mix with basic art of (such such as musical instruments) The band was required to perform in solitude.

On a sunny spring day they decided to take a break in a glade of forest into the mountains, where they would not be seen. The trek into the glade is lengthy and steep, however the instrument cases that have been bound by specific effects are smaller than what they are which is why no one felt uncomfortable about their walk and the site was perfect. An easy stage was erected at the heart of the glade thanks to the casting of the brass section and the group began setting their instruments.

The defenses of the kingdom were in good shape to that point, however nearby kingdoms were attacked from marauders in roving bands over the course of the month. To keep a safe distance one of the trumpeters was bringing along his younger brother as a guard. Eddoard did not have a lot of experience in music and was not aware of rhythm. But the fact that he was an apprentice of the Wizard of the House and was familiar with fundamental abilities. When the band began getting ready, he changed to a blue jay as he took off to the summit of the tree that was tallest within the glade.

The group was practicing to celebrate the 18th birthday celebration of the oldest prince Boris and he was due to be declared Crown Prince in front of people in his role as the father's inheritor. This was a more significant event than any event that the group has played before the event, and it was custom-made music that have been written specifically for this occasion. All of the group knew the brand new tunes by heart as well as their performance of the anthem for the kingdom had been awarded a medal but conductor Bastian believed that there were some subtleties in the performance that could be improved. Magical elements added to the difficulties, as magic spells need to be created careful to prevent getting caught by the mighty Wizards who were expected to attend the celebration. The performers were lost in their quest to be perfect in each word and spell they conjure.

The only Raisha was in the corner behind with her hands resting on her lyre as she waited her turn and heard the startled squawk that a blue jay made over the music. She looked upwards. Eddoard dropped down from his tree before turning back into a young man, screaming at them to pay attention. "The kingdom is in danger! Werewolves are on their way to this area!"

The musicians jumped onto their feet and sat down, holding their instruments to their shaky frames. "We must flee," Samnor stated by securing the straps of his drum over his head.

"We can bring nothing with us," Bastian declared and pointed at the hillsides nearby. "The earth will shelter our possessions until we come back for these items. There must be a cave that is opened."

Through the discipline they learned from their years of study they calmly put away their instruments and made a massive opening into the rock. Women kneeled and asked for forgiveness from the mountain as they carried their belongings inside. The hole was then sealed and wrapped with pendants of security, and all looked around, trying in order to leave a lasting impression on the forest their minds, since there was no way to leave a trace that could alert other.

And then, as one, all the group changed into a group of deer and raced down the sides of the mountain without requirement for trails made by humans.

In the middle of the forest, they came across an urban area. With the trees in full view and bushes, they reverted to their original forms once again and walked towards the gate. It appeared like it was closed for the first since the ages. "Who goes there?" asked a guard at the wall.

Samnor stood up with his wide hands. "My colleagues and I worry about that we will be attacked. We beg for shelter."

"How do I know you're not the marauders trying to trick us?"

"You can plainly see we bear no arms," Bastian declared, however Samnor reached out to stop his steps.

"We have all been Salorevarian born and raised. If we were wary of being savage werewolves, you can tell us apart by our eyebrows of such a thickness that they frequently are positioned to meet at mid-air."

The guard was leaning toward the forward. "I think you're correct. Head to the tower, and I'll let you in through the door to the side."

The man sat and looked at the crowd when they came in, and then apologized. "I have always believed that werewolves had hands with hairy fingers, but they don't have those. We can't say for certain today."

Raisha smiled. "You did your job. We do not take offense."

The guard yelled. He pointed at the street that was deserted. "The townspeople have locked up, so you'd better try the chapel," the priest declared. "It's the most effective defense we have. Make three knocks, and then wait for 2 more times, and Father Lagabhav's going to let into the room."

"Thank you," Samnor told the crowd, while everyone else smiled.

Eddoard protested when they led him toward the church. "I know a few battle spells."

"You won't be needing them," told his brother Neric.

"Why not? They need help in guarding their houses! Many of us can be a target for any of the criminals. The chapel's sanctity is unwise."

Bastian did a push. "Enough. We can't reveal who we are." He outlined the necessary method of knocking on the door. Then a amazed old man opened the door to welcome them.

"I was thinking we'd had everyone else already. Ah! Lady Juliet!" he said and recognized some of the players on clarinet. "I was unaware that there was a lady here. You're welcome to bring in, My Grace." He turned back out from the building, bowing more strongly than is normal from these joints in order to expose the dark internals of the house.

Samnor seemed surprised, however the rest of the band parted in order to let Juliet through. She slipped back behind her as an group of friends. Samnor followed her to the rear as the doors closed behind them.

"This was not a planned visit, Father," Juliet stated. "I was driving through the area at the time I got warnings of attack. The other musicians I know and I need refuge from your sanctuaries If you're willing to accept it."

"Of course, of course!" Father Lagabhav bows once more. "We aren't able to provide the appropriate accommodation for your Grace. But I'd certainly not refuse to accommodate my Lord's daughter. I'll need you to explain the things you've done in the past six years. Are you still in this band?"

Samnor laughed and snorted. Juliet tried to hide her face. "I believe of it that your father will have sent his sincerest regards if be aware that I'd be seeing you. In terms of the lodgings I'll be content with whatever is secured. My bodyguards are competent but I am still afraid of those creatures who harass us."

"I think you'll all fit in my secret room," the priest declared taking an unlit candle from the nearby holders and walking down the hallway. "It's pretty, but it's also hidden so you don't have to be concerned about it. The house hasn't been burgled or damaged, unless it was a case of criminals. I put our Prince Boris in the area a couple of years in the past, as His Majesty was worried that there could be assassins in the area, but the prince didn't suffer a scratch."

In a room for storage in a storage room, Father Lagabhav lifted up the rug to reveal the trapdoor. He opened it and went through a set of steps that led to down to the basement. The group followed swiftly, as there was only one illumination. The path took many abrupt turns and numerous branches that went off in different directions, which they didn't take. Sometimes they traversed the edges of massive caves that were inky black and was not able to be broken by the tiny flame. The entire area beneath the town was a maze.

Samnor who was the highest, required a squat when the passages were narrower. "Who is going to guide us back after the ordeal has ended? We won't be able find the way to return on our own."

"I've got to protect the inner sanctuary," Father Lagabhav stated. "Don't be worried, I'll be there for you once the process is over. Nobody else can tell you the exact way to go."

He finally stopped at the wooden entrance placed in the rock. He then took out a huge key ring. "You'll be safe here, milady."

The bedroom was as shabby and dingy like the picture, with two beds and some chairs. Father Lagabhav pulled out a chest from beneath on one bed. He was able to open it up to expose a stash of flint as well as candles. "You'll be tempted to take the candles. There's food in the second candle." He started the first candle, and gave it to Samnor before rushing to the exit. The door closed in front of him and, before anybody could stop him there was a click sound from the bolt breaking through the lock.

Samnor knocked out the flame and lit the area with a ball lighting. "He has effectively trapped us."

Eddoard held his hands over the door. "We should break out of here and fight!"

"No," Bastian said. "We were looking for safety and this is the most secure option we have. We'll wait to wait to see what is happening."

The males were not able to sit down on the bed, and left them unoccupied for women. Bastian and Eddoard received chairs while the rest of them were forced to sit on the floor. There was only Samnor was standing and resting on the wall in front of the door and displaying a discontented expression. Nobody spoke throughout the lengthy time.

After three hours, Eddoard looked up. "I would like to see you content. I will not issue any further warnings."

Nobody else was connected to the magical alarm system that was in place for the kingdom. As a result, there was no way to verify the claim, however they believed the young man. Juliet was asleep and off, woke up and the two were watching the front door eagerly awaiting Father Lagabhav's arrival.

The wait continued for an time. "How long can it take him to find his way here again?" Raisha told them at the end.

Samnor looked grim. "He was well-versed in the route. The journey took only twenty minutes for us to arrive at this location. It should have been there at this point." Bastian stood up. "We must get ourselves outside. Do you know how to open doors?"

Neric was able to get into the gate, and within minutes they were within the doorway. "Now what do we do?"

"I might be able to recall the way back," Samnor stated, turning toward the left. The others followed, all striving to help in the hunt for the right way. Initially, it appeared as that they could make it eventually, but soon they discovered themselves inside a cave that no one was able to remember the last time they were there the cave, and then they began argument.

Bastian stood up and held out an arm to indicate silence. "This is a mistake. Do you have any other suggestions?"

Raisha was able to close her eyes and with a frown, concentrating. "Let no one breathe for just a moment." Everybody took a deep breath. The woman looked back. "I am able to locate the closest source of air freshness. It could be an entry point."

"Let's test to do that. Be the example," Samnor said.

The route Raisha was taking them along wasn't familiar however, it soon began to rise upwards, and they began to feel more hopeful. Finally, they found the door that they'd never had before seen. By it was clear that everyone could smell fresh air rushing in beneath the door. The woman tried opening the door. The knob turned however, the door moved only a little bit before hitting something that stopped it.

Samnor approached her and yelled. "I can handle this." He positioned his shoulder towards the door, and then began pushing. The lightbulb flickered however, the door slammed shut followed by a flood of light throughout the hallway.

The door opened to the room, which was lavishly furnished. The floor to the left of the door was a bookcase that had fallen over, probably concealing the hidden passage. The hearth was where a fire was burning, however it was starting to die down.

Bastian entered the room, walking carefully across the bookcase before throwing another wood on the hearth. Through a few feint movements of the poker just like his conductor's baton set it ablaze in a fiery flame. The entire room was lit in order for the musicians to be seen as they walked out.

Juliet exclaimed in shock at the moment she was first person to see the horrific image. Within the space was a bed that was filled with the dismembered corpses of the entire family. Everyone looked up at the thing that the clarinet player was looking at, but the majority of them turned away and walked away. The area was unaffected.

The word that was never spoken was suspended in the air like the blade of a spider's thread marauders. Werewolves. Murderers. They were speechless and rushed out and into the home. The front door was open sitting on the floor in the kitchen. The cold wind was blowing through the gap it left in its wake.

"Search for survivors," Bastian declared, and with silence, they left towards the darkening darkness. The town was exactly the same as previously, with the exception of one or two bodies of a ex-guard on the road. Every single house that they saw had windows or doors cut off and the people in their homes dead without a trace of struggle. The door of Father Lagabhav was torn open at the foot of his chapel.

They yelled out to anyone people who could have hidden in the same way, and in the absence of a response, Juliet looked around to see if there was any evidence of life. But all they saw was a cat, who'd got caught inside a container. There were no other creatures in the area as the cat sprinted through the rubble of the gate after he was freed.

Eddoard raised his head when the message he received was not heard. "The army has arrived," Eddoard said. "They are able to defeat the rebels. They are now running across the border to Collumna which is home to the Collumna army, which is being notified. The werewolves will be captured."

Chapter 8: The New Girl

Charlotte as well as her peers stared at the girl who was new. Briar looked at her with a smug expression, in a way as if she felt resentful at the way Mrs. Appleton had put a warm hand around her shoulders. Briar had fair skin and a sad facial expression. Her hair was a wild that was an odd color of lavender-gray Charlotte was not used to seeing before her. It was loose and wild on her face.

The eyes of her were big and greenish yellow. The eyebrows of her were black while her chin curled towards a sharp point and her legs and arms were small and slim. The model wore a flowing, violet dress that was out of fashion, featuring purple-striped leggings as well as large black boots that slid against the floor as she was walking.

Looking at Briar Thorncliffe's face caused Charlotte chills. And she knew that other classmates also felt the same. However, they all robotically stated, "Welcome, Briar" with a single voice as they knew Mrs. Appleton would be upset If they didn't.

Briar was unable to do anything except stared at her group, and a smile in her light-colored eyes. She finally was seated at her desk it was just to the left of Charlotte.

Charlotte shivered. Charlotte didn't want Briar close to her, but she knew she needed to get the most out of the situation. Inducing a smile as she looked over, she smiled and said "Hi" to the new girl.

Briar was the only one to glare back at her.

In reality, Briar was so icy towards the whole class that by recess the class had not even dared to contact her. Charlotte as well as her classmates kept their distance, and they were playing their own games, while Briar was swaying with the winds of autumn skipping and sliding through the field of soccer that had been swept by the wind.

"Why is she dancing like that?" Charlotte's best friend Tommy was curious.

"She looks like a creepy kid from a horror movie!" said Destiny.

Charlotte did a smile. "I wish we had a normal new girl in our class!"

The next few days, the entire world did not stop to think about Briar. This was the only thing they could do. If they attempted to talk with Briar, Briar was hostile and not friendly. Briar was never one to be a part of the others in the class during activities and gym or recess.

However, the more students claimed she was not there the more Briar Thorncliffe was noticed. The dancer continued to perform her eccentric routine in recess, spinning as she whirled towards the play area, so that the children were aware of her. At times, she would climb over the trees' peaks and then sing a deep and haunting tune until the supervising teacher called her to come down. And then, everyone laughed, and her bright eyes flashed at the sight of fury.

"It's like she wants us to pay attention to her," Charlotte said in the afternoon. "But she doesn't want to do anything with us."

"She sure is weird," Tommy responded.

In the evening of Halloween the Mrs. Appleton threw a festive event for her students which included a unique halloween version of show and tell. Charlotte and her classmates had a blast.

Charlotte disguised herself as a gypsy and brought along her mother's unique pendant to showing and telling. It came all across Spain together with her great-grandparents. Charlotte believed it was an ideal piece of jewelry to display.

Briar Thorncliffe was dressed up as the role of a witch wearing her dark purple, and a the pointed witch's cap over her head. In her presentation the actress brought along her black cat Magic.

It was not thought by anyone Briar's dress was something from a movie. However, Briar seemed at home wearing her costume because it seemed to reflect her true self.

While Briar displayed her cat at show-and-tell Destiny was able to get closer Charlotte and said "If I didn't know any better, I'd say that Briar was a real witch and that Magic was a real witch's cat."

In that exact moment it was to be so silent. It was clear that the sound of a pin dropping. Briar looked her fierce yellow eye at Destiny and inquired "What was that you said?"

"N-nothing," Destiny stammered.

"Don't lie to me!" Briar's voice was in a shrill tone, like it frequently would during her haunting tunes.

"Briar--" Mrs. Appleton began.

"And don't interrupt me!" Everyone screamed as Briar corrected her teacher with the most stern, cold voice.

"I've had about enough of being whispered about and ignored," Briar was roaring on with her pet on her shoulder. "And so I've decided that now is the time to give Magic a special Halloween treat!"

In a single whispered word and an elongated hand, Briar transformed Mrs. Appleton, Charlotte, and her friends into a group of skittering, scurrying white mice!

"Bon appetite, Magic!" smiled Briar.

Charlotte Mouse looked around at her friends' mouse eyes in utter despair. The mouse friends knew now they were all aware that Briar Thorncliffe was an actual witch. And that this, with no an possibility, was also the final Halloween that any of them will ever get to experience!

Just to have fun!

Create a pumpkin with paint to make it make it look as Briar Thorncliffe's cat. Magic!

It is recommended to have:

One mini pumpkin

Paint in black

Paint brush

Craft foam

Scissors

glue

Neon yellow or green construction paper

Permanent marker with metallic color.

Get an adult to purchase your a miniature pumpkin. (These can be found in craft shops and at the grocery store throughout the fall.)

The mini pumpkin is painted completely in black.

Let dry.

After the paint has dried after drying, cut two triangles from craft foam.

The triangles can be glued to the inside of the pumpkin to make the cat's ears.

Then, cut two circular pieces of neon-green or yellow construction paper to make cats' eyes. Put them on top of each other then add two more black circles made of foam to form eyes.

Attach an orange triangle under the eyes to create the appearance of a cat's nose.

Utilize a metallic gold silver permanent marker, or a white one for drawing whiskers on the cat's pumpkin.

Meow!

No Joke

"Do I really have to play with that new kid?" Paul was adamant to his parents on a sunny late afternoon on a Saturday in October. "He's cruel to everyone and he doesn't smile. One of the only times he makes a joke is to tell us that he'll cook stew out of us should you do anything that upsets him."

Paul's mom was kind enough to give him a handshake. "I know it can be hard when other kids aren't nice," she told him. "But I'm convinced that should you and your peers are willing to give Herbie the chance to prove yourself to be honest, you'll see he's good. Herbie's bark could be more destructive than his bite. It's likely that he's being anxious and frightened because there aren't any other playmates in the area yet."

Paul looked at his feet and sighed. He wasn't convinced about the matter.

Herbie had been living in the area since last August and it didn't appear to Paul as if he had any intention to get any kind of acquaintances. Actually, it wasn't like he seemed to be doing anything other than give other children an earful!

"Go on, Paul," the father advised, while gently pointing him towards the front door. "It's an ideal day to stay inside. Enjoy some time with your buddies Later, Mom and I'll take your shopping for your costume for Halloween. We'll then all meet up to eat pizza."

There's always something I can look forward to, Paul thought. Paul walked out to the bright, crisp autumnal day. The vibrant fallen leaves along the pavement squeaked on his toes, and at once, Paul could not help but smile. It could be that today wasn't so horrible at all. Perhaps Herbie was busy and maybe he'd not be able to join Paul as well as his buddies!

The thought caused Paul accelerate his steps. He ran across the street, and then down an alley that ran through center of block. On one end of the alley, was an enormous empty parking space which the kids of the neighborhood loved to meet. There was even an basketball court there.

Yes, Paul's buddies Eric, Tyler, Carlos, Rachel, and Jackie were also present. However, they weren't the only ones there. Herbie was also present as well. Paul could see from the expressions on children's faces that he had been giving everyone the utmost difficulty, just like every other day.

In the way that kids are, Herbie was quite unattractive. He had a sour greenish appearance to his pale skin He also had massive black bags that hung over his eyes. The day before, he was wearing grey T-shirts with the image of a skull as well as a slingshot, a gun as well as a rock.

"Hi, Paul!" Paul's pals phoned.

"Hey, you guys!" cried Paul.

Herbie has just muted something in his mouth.

Recalling the words his parents stated, Paul drew a deep breath, then turned his attention toward the child. Paul wanted to help Herbie feel comfortable, and especially in the event that it would get rid of his mental health issues.

"That's a pretty cool slingshot you've got there, Herbie," He said with a smile. "Mind if I try it?"

Herbie shook his head darkly. "I'll make stew out of you if you make me mad!" He cautioned. "And playing with my slingshot will definitely make me mad!"

Paul left. "Okay, okay. You can choose. I just wanted to know."

However, Rachel the rough and tumble girl, took a step forward with her baseball cap tucked on top of her long brown braids. "You know what, Herbie?" she inquired. "That comedy about stew is becoming old! Who do you think would be if you were to bully us this way?"

"Yeah!" chimed Carlos and he sided with Rachel.

"Yeah!" echoed Paul in awe of his fellow comrades.

"Yeah!" chorused the other.

Herbie's face grew darker to a stunning hue of purple. His eyes swung crazy as his voice rang out with a loud scream. "You asked for it!" he mumbled. after that, he pulled back his slingshot, and sent the sharp rock towards Paul and his fellow comrades.

Chapter 9: The Kids Immediately Began

The kids were so awestruck and couldn't even move. They could barely move. Paul was able to feel his heart beat in fear when Herbie grasped all the youngsters by the hand and began to drag them along the street with a superhuman force.

"I'll have my mother cook you all up into a delicious stew for my lunch!" Herbie laughed wildly. "You see, kids, it wasn't a joke, after all!"

"Mr. Napper's Cape

"You asked who to babysit us tonight?" Kyle was stunned, gazing at his mother with wild eyes in disbelief.

"Mr. Napper,"" she mumbled as she walked closer to the mirror of her dresser to apply her mascara effectively. "Honestly, Kyle, I don't know why you're getting yourself so worked-up over this."

"Because!" Kyle spat. "Mr. Napper is a dangerous person! Everybody knows this! He watched Greg's young cousins and nobody has ever heard from them. "Mr. Napper is a kidnapper Mama!"

Kyle's mom threw her mascara in her makeup bag, and then began to play with her hair. She lifted and spraying it effortlessly. "You're a smart boy, Kyle," she said to her son. "You certainly know better than to judge people by their names!"

At times, Kyle simply didn't get it. mother's. She seemed to be concerned a lot more about her appearance more than other things, specifically her own children! "Didn't you hear what I said about Greg's cousins?" He inquired.

His mother waved her hands with a sneer. "That wasn't Mr. Napper's fault. Twins ran out of their bedroom windows and sped off. This was tragic, but what could he possibly had known? Don't give the old man an opportunity!"

"I will not!" Kyle was furious. "Greg says that Mr. Napper wears a long, magical red cape that makes kids disappear!"

The mother of Greg was reaching for hairspray when she heard the sound of laughter filling her voice. "You as well as Greg are too imaginative! "Mr. Napper is a retired magician for sure however, he's not really amazing. He doesn't even make children disappear." The woman spritzed her blonde, platinum hair to the point that the entire room was sprayed with hairspray.

Kyle was coughing and moved off the reflection. "Then why didn't anyone ever find Greg's cousins?" He questioned.

"You know how it goes, hun!" The boy's mother put necklaces on necklaces and secured them on her neck. "Not every child missing is located. Even though I'd hate not to acknowledge it, there isn't an end-to-end happy ending for all stories around the globe!"

She smiled brightly red, lipstick-colored smile at Kyle and walked away from the room amid the haze of hairspray, and perfume.

It's not going to be a happy end for our tale, too, Kyle thought grimly. Kyle knew that it was his responsibility to be watchful for himself and his little brother Landon as their mother went to the fall fashion show on in the evening with her newest girlfriend.

"Mr. Napper showed up at six o'clock at the latest. He was just like the weird, spooky appearance Greg has described. He had the most massive nose, the longest Kyle could have ever had, and he was wearing an official top hat his head. However, the thing that stood out to him was the length of his flowing, red cape that which he was wearing over his clothes.

The cape that disappeared from the kid! Kyle was thinking with a shiver.

"What adorable children!" Mr. Napper gushed in a low nasal tone, staring smugly to Kyle as well as Landon.

Kyle did a face and his mom seemed attracted by Mr. Napper's appealing charm. "Why, thank you!" she exclaimed. "See y'all later!" Then the woman was gone.

"Well, boys." Mr. Napper turned to Kyle as well as his brother. "What will we do first? Should we sit down to food? Have a read? or play with hide-and-seek?"

Kyle was thinking fast. As he snatched Landon to his chest, Kyle said "Let's play hide-and-seek." The idea was to provide them with a chance to get away.

It was a bad decision.

With a smile from ear-to-ear He was so happy that Napper was giggling from ear to ear. Napper cried, "Perfect! Then I've just the location to keep you two!" With that, He threw his cloth over the heads of the boys and black, glistening glittering dust floated around the two boys!

Then, they could feel themselves sliding, falling before falling into a slick dark vortex! The baby Landon was screaming, and Kyle attempted to hold onto his younger brother, but he fell from his arms and soared through the darkness!

Once they landed, Kyle and Landon found themselves in a blurred blue world dotted with a plethora of kids. Many were crying, others were screaming, while others had a silent, stoned face.

Kyle grabbed a terrified newborn Landon in his lap. Kyle exclaimed when he saw Greg's twin cousins Layla as well as Jannie.

"Layla!" he cried. "Jannie!"

"Kyle!" the twins shouted.

"Don't tell me Mr. Napper got you, too?" Jannie asked.

Kyle looked at him with a grim smile. "Where are we?" Kyle would like to know.

"We're in his cape," told Layla The answer was what Kyle was afraid of.

Kyle's heart was pounding with terror. "If only Mom had listened to me!" Kyle shouted. "How do we get out of here?"

Jannie shook her head sadly. "Don't you know?" she asked casually. "There's nothing we can do to escape. The situation is adrift for the time."

Kyle began to speak and began screaming.

The scream continued for a long time.

Just to have fun!

The Mr. Napper has a magical cape. Find out how to perform a unique magical trick that'll amaze you and your pals!

You'll need:

Box of crayons

Another person who can do this trick

Send your child a set of crayons.

Reverse your attention to your friend, and then ask them to select one of the crayons from the box.

After he or she is satisfied, place both of hands in front of you and then ask them to hold the crayon in your hands. (Remember to not move around when you are performing this trick!)

By keeping your hands in your back, inform your friend you'll know the color of crayon picked by feeling the crayon!

This is the most difficult part. While your partner isn't looking you, rub a small amount of crayon wax onto the right thumb.

Turn around and look at your friend while keeping your hands in place and keep the pencil behind you.

Move your hand towards the face of your friend and act as if listening to their thoughts. When you've done this, look at the shade you smudged off of your right thumb.

Inform your friend "I'm taking note of your thoughts! Abracadabra! The color you picked is _____!"

Chapter 10: The Scarecrow

"Whatever you do," Mr. Graves told Lizzie and her companions, "don't you dare go near the pumpkin patch on All Hallows Eve!"

It was a beautiful autumn day, with a sunny, warm weather which meant that Lizzie, Clare, and Marisol were out in the patch of pumpkins with an assortment of classmates from the school. When they came across the perfect pumpkins they planned to bring the ones back to Lizzie's place and cut out jack-o'lanterns.

The Mr. Graves, who owned the path for pumpkins, appeared to be making a huge large fuss over little. He looked funny, small-sized old man who stooped over with large, wild gray hair with dark eyes that were the shade of stormy skies. He was always dramatic and serious at Halloween. During that time, the way he behaved was particularly dramatic.

At the moment, for example He was attempting, but failing to make Lizzie along with her pals with a worn-out scarecrow at the center of the patch of pumpkins. He looked friendly wearing a cheerful head of a pumpkin, hand-held gardening gloves from the past as well as a body constructed out of old clothes filled with straw. The shoes of an ancient era--probably Mr. Graves'--sat on the ankles of his worn-out jeans.

"Mr. Graves," said Lizzie with a stern voice "do you intend to inform me you think that this spooky creature builds himself each fall, year after year, with no assistance whatsoever from your side?" She bit her lip in order to not laugh. The tale that the man. Graves had just finished to them was simply way too much!

"That is precisely what I mean, young lady," Mr. Graves replied, unsmiling. "Every October He puts his body together through sheer determination. Evil forces, I tell you! The black magic!" The wind ruffled Mr. Graves' gray hair and made it move wild.

"And furthermore," Clare continued in a similar fashion to Lizzie's teacher style, "do you mean to say that this harmless-looking scarecrow comes alive on Halloween night and chases after victims?"

"And," Marisol finished, "that he uses his very own scarecrow stake just like a dagger and drives it right through the hearts of unsuspecting little kids?"

The girls broke into giggles and giggling, but the man. Graves furrowed his brow and was looking at them with a dark look. "Believe what you wish, young ladies!" He shouted. "But one way or another, I hope you will take heed and keep away from the pumpkin patch on All Hallows Eve!" Then he swung his head to walk off.

"He's crazy!" Lizzie wept with a grin, shaking her head.

"No kidding!" said Marisol. "Is that what happens to people who never get married?"

Clare smiled. "Come on, you guys, let's pick out our pumpkins!"

The three girls spent remaining afternoon enjoying the opportunity to decorate pumpkins at Lizzie's place along with about a dozen others from the school. With the fun, they were able to forget everything concerning the infamous Mr. Graves and his bizarre advice about Halloween pumpkins.

until Halloween night, which is. Lizzie, Clare, and Marisol in costume as rock stars of their preferred girl group, been making rounds in Lizzie and Marisol's neighbourhood. They were now heading into the neighborhood of Clare to pick up yet more sweets.

In the process they passed through the Mr. Graves' pumpkin patch and saw a scarecrow lone within the field. It was illuminated by the night's light.

Clare grasped Lizzie's arm. "Oooh!" she cried in a teasing way. "It's the scarecrow with haunts! Better hurry, otherwise we could be snatched by him!"

Lizzie and Marisol were laughing. After that, Lizzie took a step back and said "You are right? I'm not worried about the Mr. Graves and his dumb tales! I'm headed to the pumpkin patch to prove to the man that his scarecrow was only a bag filled with straw!"

"Lizzie!" gasped her acquaintances. "Are you serious?"

"Why is that"?' Lizzie asked casually. "Don't tell me you believe Mr. Graves!" After that, sporting her hair-do-rock-star-style moving in the air, Lizzie ran right up to the scarecrow that was in center of the patch.

Clare and Marisol ran through the fields at Marisol's heels.

As she reached out to hold the scarecrow Lizzie was able to look at her companions and exclaimed, "See? It's just a normal scarecrow! You can wait until tomorrow in which I will inform him that Mr. Graves how wrong he was!"

Her friends were expected to laugh and be happy and agree, however Clare and Marisol simply stood in shock, mouths open in awe and looked at something that was directly in front of Lizzie.

Lizzie frowned. "What is it, you guys?" Lizzie swiveled her neck to examine herself, and she screamed!

There, just in front of Lizzie, stood a scarecrow who had become a real person! He no longer appeared at you as if he was friendly and innocent. The huge, gaping face was filled with a gaping pit of terror as his tiny pumpkin eyes were sharp and intimidating. And, the worst part was that he been able to climb down from his stake, and used it as an axe, pointing straight towards the girl!

"Run!" Lizzie shrieked.

Then she felt the intense, searing pain that was piercing into her heart.

Poor Lizzie fell to the floor and took her last breath.

Even that Clare or Marisol dissented, they couldn't avoid the eagle, neither.

The morning of the first of November the late Mr. Graves found the bodies of his three closest buddies in his patch of pumpkins. "Such a shame," Mr. Graves said in a husky voice. "If only they had taken heed!"

Just for fun!

Create your own easy Halloween scarecrow!

You'll need:

Paper bag in brown

Newspaper

Tape

Pencil

Construction paper

Scissors